MW01225340

Practical Issues in Collection Development and Collection Access

The 1993 Charleston Conference

Practical Issues
in Collection Development
and Collection Access
The 1993
Charleston Conference

Katina Strauch
Sally Somers
Susan Zappen
Anne Jennings
Editors

Withdrawn

OCT 12 2024

UNBC Library

UNBC LIBRARY

The Haworth Press, Inc.
New York · London

Practical Issues in Collection Development and Collection Access: The 1993 Charleston Conference has also been published as *Collection Management*, Volume 19, Numbers 3/4 1995.

© 1995 by The Haworth Press, Inc. All rights reserved. No part of this work may be reproduced or utilized in any form or by any means, electronic or mechanical, including photocopying, microfilm and recording, or by any information storage and retrieval system, without permission in writing from the publisher. Printed in the United States of America.

The development, preparation, and publication of this work has been undertaken with great care. However, the publisher, employees, editors, and agents of The Haworth Press and all imprints of The Haworth Press, Inc., including The Haworth Medical Press and Pharmaceutical Products Press, are not responsible for any errors contained herein or for consequences that may ensue from use of materials or information contained in this work. Opinions expressed by the author(s) are not necessarily those of The Haworth Press, Inc.

The Haworth Press, Inc., 10 Alice Street, Binghamton, NY 13904-1580

Library of Congress Cataloging-in-Publication Data

Practical issues in collection development and collection access : the 1993 Charleston Conference / Katina Strauch . . . [et al.].
    p. cm.
Includes bibliographical references and index.
ISBN 1-56024-733-9 (alk. paper)
    1. Collection development (Libraries–United States–Congresses. 2. Academic libraries–Collection development–United States–Congresses. 3. Indexing–United States–Congresses. I. Strauch, Katina P., 1946- .
Z687.2.U6P73 1995
025.2'1877–dc20
                                                      95-16712
                                                      CIP

INDEXING & ABSTRACTING

Contributions to this publication are selectively indexed or abstracted in print, electronic, online, or CD-ROM version(s) of the reference tools and information services listed below. This list is current as of the copyright date of this publication. See the end of this section for additional notes.

- *Current Awareness Bulletin*, Association for Information Management, Information House, 20-24 Old Street, London, EC1V 9AP, England

- *Index to Periodical Articles Related to Law*, University of Texas, 727 East 26th Street, Austin, TX 78705

- *Information Reports & Bibliographies*, Science Associates International, Inc., 465 West End Avenue, New York, NY 10024

- *Information Science Abstracts*, Plenum Publishing Company, 233 Spring Street, New York, NY 10013-1578

- *Informed Librarian, The*, Infosources Publishing, 140 Norma Road, Teaneck, NJ 07666

- *INTERNET ACCESS (& additional networks) Bulletin Board for Libraries ("BUBL"), coverage of information resources on INTRENET, JANET, and other networks.*
  - JANET X.29: UK.AC.BATH.BUBL or 00006012101300
  - TELNET: BUBL.BATH.AC.UK or 138.38.32.45 login 'bubl'
  - Gopher: BUBL.BATH.AC.UK (138.32.32.45). Port 7070
  - World Wide Web: http: / / www.bubl.bath.ac.uk./BUBL/ home.html
  - NISSWAIS telnetniss.ac.uk (for the NISS gateway)
  The Andersonian Library, Curran Building, 101 St. James Road, Glasgow G4 ONS, Scotland

- *Library & Information Science Abstracts (LISA)*, Bowker-Saur Limited, Maypole House, Maypole Road, East Grinstead, West Sussex, RH19 1HH, England

- *Library Hi Tech News*, Pierian Press, P.O. Box 1808, Ann Arbor, MI 48106

(continued)

- *Library Literature*, The H.W. Wilson Company, 950 University Avenue, Bronx, NY 10452

- *OT BibSys*, American Occupational Therapy Foundation, P.O. Box 1725, Rockville, MD 20849-1725

- *PASCAL International Bibliography T205: Sciences de l'information Documentation*, INIST/CNRS-Service Gestion des Documents Primaires, 2, allee du Parc de Brabois, F-54514 Vandoeuvre-les-Nancy, Cedex, France

- *Referativnyi Zhurnal (Abstracts Journal of the Institute of Scientific Information of the Republic of Russia)*, The Institute of Scientific Information, Baltijskaja ul., 14, Moscow, A-219, Republic of Russia

Book reviews are selectively excerpted by the Guide to Professional Literature of the Journal of Academic Librarianship.

SPECIAL BIBLIOGRAPHIC NOTES

related to special journal issues (separates)
and indexing / abstracting

☐ indexing/abstracting services in this list will also cover material in any "separate" that is co-published simultaneously with Haworth's special thematic journal issue or DocuSerial. Indexing/abstracting usually covers material at the article/chapter level.

☐ monographic co-editions are intended for either non-subscribers or libraries which intend to purchase a second copy for their circulating collections.

☐ monographic co-editions are reported to all jobbers/wholesalers/approval plans. The source journal is listed as the "series" to assist the prevention of duplicate purchasing in the same manner utilized for books-in-series.

☐ to facilitate user/access services all indexing/abstracting services are encouraged to utilize the co-indexing entry note indicated at the bottom of the first page of each article/chapter/contribution.

☐ this is intended to assist a library user of any reference tool (whether print, electronic, online, or CD-ROM) to locate the monographic version if the library has purchased this version but not a subscription to the source journal.

☐ individual articles/chapters in any Haworth publication are also available through the Haworth Document Delivery Services (HDDS).

Practical Issues in Collection Development and Collection Access

The 1993 Charleston Conference

CONTENTS

ABOUT THE EDITORS

Katina Strauch, MLS, is Head, Collection Development, at the College of Charleston Libraries where she has been employed since 1979. She is the founder of the internationally acclaimed Charleston Conference: Issues in Book and Serial Acquisition, which began in 1980, and is the editor of the international trade journal *Against the Grain.* Ms. Strauch was the recipient of the UNC-Chapel Hill SILS Distinguished Alumna Award in May of 1992. She has published widely in the professional literature.

Sally W. Somers has been Assistant University Librarian for Technical Services at Tulane University since 1989. She is active in the American Library Association and has served on several committees in the Association for Library Collections and Technical Services. Ms. Somers has published in several journals and is on the book review panel for *Library Acquisitions: Practice and Theory.*

Susan Zappen is Acquisitions and Serials Librarian at Folsom Library at Rensselaer Polytechnic Institute in Troy, New York. A graduate of the University of Missouri, she has been affiliated with several university libraries in addition to serving as a library consultant. Since 1991 she has been a presenter at the Charleston Conference preconference on serials.

Anne F. Jennings, MLIS, is a law librarian with the firm of Sinkler & Boyd in Charleston, South Carolina. She also serves as Assistant to the Editor of *Against the Grain* and authors several columns which appear in that publication. Ms. Jennings is a member of the American Association of Law Libraries and the Special Libraries Association.

ALL HAWORTH BOOKS AND JOURNALS
ARE PRINTED ON CERTIFIED
ACID-FREE PAPER

Introduction

Katina Strauch

They came, they saw, they learned. Four hundred thirty-eight people (67 publishers, 63 vendors, 8 consultants, and 300 librarians) participated to make the thirteenth Charleston Conference on November 4-6, 1993, a success. In the midst of the sea air and refreshing history that surrounds Charleston, this mix of professionals approached the evolving world of information selection, maintenance, access and delivery with creative energy, intellectual rigor, and growing expertise in areas that we didn't know existed when the Conference was first founded. The span of years between 1980, when the first Charleston Conference was held, and 1994, has seen incredible changes in librarianship and in the world of information selection and maintenance as well as in information access and delivery. This evolving landscape was the meat of the 1993 Charleston Conference. In this volume are produced twelve of the papers that comprised the 1993 Charleston Conference. Below, we have attempted to give you an overview of the entire Conference.

The 1993 Charleston Conference began with three preconferences held on Wednesday afternoon. These dealt with serials cancellation (Buzzy Basch, coordinator), managing acquisitions (Janet Flowers, UNC-Chapel Hill, and Suzanne Striedick, N.C. State University, coordinators), and the art of negotiation (Paul Clipp, presenter, Judy Luther, Faxon, and John Secor, Yankee Book Peddler, coordinators). These excellent preconferences were a mix of the old (serial cancellations), the new (negotiation), and the evolving (managing acquisitions).

[Haworth co-indexing entry note]: "Introduction." Strauch, Katina. Co-published simultaneously in *Collection Management* (The Haworth Press, Inc.) Vol. 19, Nos. 3/4, 1995, pp. 1-5; and: *Practical Issues in Collection Development and Collection Access: The 1993 Charleston Conference* (ed: Katina Strauch et al.) The Haworth Press, Inc., 1995, pp. 1-5. Multiple copies of this article/chapter may be purchased from The Haworth Document Delivery Center [1-800-3-HAWORTH; 9:00 a.m. - 5:00 p.m. (EST)].

© 1995 by The Haworth Press, Inc. All rights reserved. *1*

After an informal reception the night before, the Conference itself began on Thursday, November 4 with a newcomers' welcome. Over the years as the Charleston Conference has evolved, it has always been rejuvenated by new perspectives. The president of the College of Charleston welcomed the group with one of his famous anecdotes. Pointing to the fact that he had just come from a meeting with a group of students clamoring for library access 24 hours a day, he said that this was a great tribute to the role of libraries and librarians in teaching the leaders of tomorrow.

With this positive perspective, led by Rosann Bazirjian (Syracuse University) and Joyce Ogburn (Yale University) we began to discuss document delivery and collection development as it is currently evolving. There are a lot of unanswered questions, but it is clear that decisions are being made which will impact our world into the twenty-first century. Chris Filstrup (George Washington University) talked about the role of Consortia from his perspective at George Washington University and from the standpoint of the emerging electronic environment. He was followed by Randy Olsen (Brigham Young University) who shared a practical approach to acquiring electronic files. Next we heard from Nancy Stanley (Penn State) about acquiring electronic journals. Anna Perrault (Florida State University), talked about the research which she has done for her Ph.D. (library science) dissertation on the national monograph collection and the changing scope of purchasing in the period 1985-1990 when library budgets were hit the hardest and cuts had to be made.

This year the Conference had several new features as the able organizer (Judy Webster, University of Tennessee) worked to bring new vitality to the Conference. Featured were Simulation Rooms in which participants could visit a situation in a work environment different from their own. As the Conference grows, participants become more and more shy about making their thoughts and opinions known. Therefore, a "talk show host" component embodied by Dick Dougherty (University of Michigan) was initiated this year. Dougherty's role was to facilitate discussion. With his usual charm and intellectual vigor, Dougherty did just that.

After nearly half of the participants partook of "lively lunches," opportunities for smaller groups to discuss topics pertinent to the world of books, journals, automation, exchange rates, and standards, we began the afternoon with an incisive paper by John Clouston (King's College, Ontario, Canada) who spoke about establishing a standard for collecting materials in disciplines. Wanda Dole (SUNY-Stony Brook) continued on the topic of collection analysis when she discussed the OCLC/Amigos Collection Analysis CD and its strengths in measuring of collection strengths and weaknesses for her library's collections. Deborah Lee (Mississippi State) expanded our view when she spoke about "paperless" acquisitions and the changes in processing brought about by electronic initiatives. This segued nicely into the EDI (Electronic Data Interchange) panel discussion next, led by Keith Schmiedl (Coutts Library Service) and including Sandy Paul (SKP Associates), Glen Kelly (Laurentian Library, Canada), and John Cox (Blackwells). The Conference ended for the day after this intensive EDI discussion and we all dined and danced in an optional cruise of Charleston Harbor for a break.

On Friday, November 5, the participants turned to the publishing scene. Despite the fact that we had heard a lot about electronic resources, there are still a lot of traditional monographs and journals being published. Colin Day (University of Michigan Press) called for more cooperation between libraries and publishers. Speaking of the decline in sales for monographs, Day alluded both to the drop in publishing in certain subject areas and to the need for a more viable publishing solution for some faculty members. The next publishers' section of the Conference featured a look at reference publishing and what librarians are looking for. Audrey Melkin (Henry Holt) and Eileen Tobin (Garland) gave us their perspectives on the current trends in reference publishing. William Russey (VCH) is a former faculty member who now works for a publishing company and he gave his perspective on the new electronic delivery of information. Finally, Ian Eastment (Sage) discussed the journals cancellation crisis and the fact that publishers will continue to publish journals which must grow and adapt to market needs or die.

After more lively lunches on Friday, participants were awakened to discuss "Contentious Issues." Featuring Lynne Rienner (Lynne Rienner Publishers), this panel covered the waterfront of discussion on some of the major issues which we confront today–copyright, access versus ownership, and fair use. The most contentious of the issues dealt with acquiring paperback versus hardcover materials and was covered ably by Carol Eyler and Beth Hammond, both of Mercer University. Matt Nauman (Blackwell North America) covered the vendor perspective on this issue and spoke to the initiatives of several vendors in this regard. In speaking of Vendor Performance, Lynne Branche Brown (Penn State) opened another contentious issue.

Friday night ended with the Conference reception at the Old Exchange Building in the middle of downtown historic Charleston. The Exchange Building is one of the most historic buildings in America.

Saturday dawned bright and clear and the day began with an international panel chaired by Julie Gelfand (UC, Irvine). "Around the World with Librarians, Publishers and Vendors," included Glen Secor (Yankee Book Peddler), Charles Germain (PCG), Rolf Hasslöw (Chalmers Institute of Technology, Sweden), Stephen Lustig (Cassell), Mary Gilles (Swets), and Digby Sales (University of Cape Town, South Africa). This far-reaching panel allowed us to consider NAFTA and the Canadian Book Trade, shrinking budgets in Swedish libraries, censorship and availability of materials in South Africa, publishing and the contrast of the competitive environment in the U.S. and U.K., and the proverbial exchange rate. Later Saturday morning, Brian Cox (Pergamon, filling in for Barbara Meyers) coordinated a marketing panel which consisted of Susan Knapp (American Psychological Association), Patricia Scarry (University of Chicago Press), and Jill O'Neill (Elsevier).

The final paper of the Conference was delivered by the inimitable Clifford Lynch (University of California, Office of the President). Presenting his vision of the future of scholarly communication, Lynch discussed how electronics might change scholarship of the future in terms of publishing, doing business, funding, integrity, control, and promotion and tenure. Leading into the ending of the Conference, Lynch raised more questions than he answered, leaving plenty of food for discussion at future Charleston Conferences.

The 1993 Charleston Conference ended amid much fanfare and good will. Once again, the participants realized that they might disagree, but that they have many of the same values and concerns about the system that drives us all. Presented here are twelve of the papers that comprised the 1993 Charleston Conference. We believe that they give an excellent look at some of the issues that face all of us as we enter into the twenty-first century. "Bubble, bubble, toil and trouble/Eye of newt and toe of frog/wool of bat and tongue of dog." No matter what you give us, we'll figure it out. And we are all in this together!

Enjoy!

A Charmed Brew:
Document Delivery
and Collection Development
in the Fast Lane

Rosann Bazirjian

"Double, double toil and trouble: fire, burn; and cauldron, bubble";[1] I smell confusion in the air. As the witches in Macbeth prepare their "charmed pot"[2] of "powerful trouble"[3] we sit here today with an array of powerful ingredients ourselves. But, unlike the witches' blend of fillet of fenny snake, eye of newt, toe of frog or even wool of bat,[4] we need to find a tasty recipe for Uncover2, ArticleFirst, Loansome Doc, Citadel, Adonis, Dialorder or how about these acronyms: UMI, IOD, NTIS, ISI, ERIC, ACS or EI; I wonder what those would conjure up. As we choose between on-site document delivery services or remote services and attempt to evaluate types of access available, costs involved, turn-around time, ease of order placement, delivery options, frequency of update, and technical support provided, we have created for ourselves not only a charmed brew, but as Ronald Leach says, "an electronic tower of Babylon."[5]

Confused? Where does the confusion lie? Not only must we choose between the services I just mentioned, but we need to decide

Rosann Bazirjian is Head of Bibliographic Services at Syracuse University Library, 123 Lake Country Drive, Syracuse, NY 13209.

[Haworth co-indexing entry note]: "A Charmed Brew: Document Delivery and Collection Development in the Fast Lane." Bazirjian, Rosann. Co-published simultaneously in *Collection Management* (The Haworth Press, Inc.) Vol. 19, Nos. 3/4, 1995, pp. 7-10; and: *Practical Issues in Collection Development and Collection Access: The 1993 Charleston Conference* (ed: Katina Strauch et al.) The Haworth Press, Inc., 1995, pp. 7-10. Multiple copies of this article/chapter may be purchased from The Haworth Document Delivery Center [1-800-3-HAWORTH; 9:00 a.m. - 5:00 p.m. (EST)].

© 1995 by The Haworth Press, Inc. All rights reserved.   7 on the system and mode of delivery as well! Will we use fax, or how about Federal Express, Overnight Courier, United Parcel Service, Next Day Air, and please don't forget Second Day Air. The option of electronic scanning also exists, and for some, Ariel is the answer, where a scanned fax is sent over the Internet. Others may model their delivery system on that which the National Agricultural Library has developed, or Ohio State University, where scanned images are received directly on a patron's work station. So I repeat, the proliferation of services and types of access available are confusing.

But believe me, the confusion does not stop here. What about our bibliographers? As patron expectations increase due to their ability to gain access to so much more information in our on-line systems, the bibliographer is faced with even more demands. There are more variables on which the subject selector must make spending decisions. As budgets shrink, and as funds dwindle due to unfavorable exchange rates and inflation, do they still stress ownership, or provide access? Coupled with these fiscal realities, the bibliographer must determine if access really *is* cheaper. As the volume of publishing increases and the size of our staffs decrease, it certainly becomes a luxury to provide both access and ownership. Yet, if they opt to provide access, which journals apply? What subscriptions can they afford to cancel? And what amount of their budget should they siphon off for document delivery? In this period of re-evaluating library collections, in this battle between traditional and alternative collection development practices, in this move to viewing the library as a "gateway of information,"[6] the bibliographer is confused.

The confusion does not stop here! What about our library administrators. The questions for them are numerous. They need to decide on *when*. Is now the time to invest in document delivery? The service is young, that is true, so how much risk is involved in making such a commitment. They also need to decide on *how*. How can the library afford it? Administrators are responsible for deciding on the pricing structure, so they need to decide if this service should be completely subsidized by the library. If not, is it ethical to charge the patron? If the library agrees to charge, due to the great variety of services available, the pricing structure can become quite complicated. Another question administrators must answer is *where*. If document delivery is the way to go, *where* should this service be located? Is this an Interlibrary Loan function, or does it more rightly belong in Reference? What about Acquisitions? What about Serials? Where should the machinery be located? And how should this new service be integrated into the work flow? Finally, administration needs to decide on the *what*, by which I mean, *what* delivery options exist. Does the library go with faxing, or electronic scanning, or a combination of the two. Does the patron receive the article directly, or should he or she be forced to come into the library to pick-up the delivered material. The potential for the library without walls is certainly here.

Now we get to the library patrons themselves. Let's look at their dilemma as they ask, where do I go for this service? Am I even eligible to use this service? Is this service only available for graduate students and faculty, or can undergraduates and the local community request articles via document delivery as well? Patrons need to ask: must I pay for this service; may I only use this service if my request is rush (and what is considered rush anyway?); can I only use this service for items which the library does not own; how many requests may I submit on a weekly, daily, or monthly basis? Surely, the patron does not have the answers, and surely, the patron is confused.

Even vendors are uncertain. The subscription agent is developing "products and services to match librarians' changing expectations."[7] Vendors are forced to re-evaluate their role in order to survive the future as they begin to expand from traditional subscription suppliers to suppliers of documents. This is necessary as libraries continue to reduce serial subscriptions. Vendors are secure in the role played as subscription agents. They are important to us: they consolidate invoices, create statistical reports, do currency conversion. Now, that security is in jeopardy. So, who do they now go to visit when they call on a library? Is it still the acquisitions or serials librarian, or is it now the interlibrary loan or reference librarian? If they get into document delivery, how do they determine pricing structures? This is the sort of confusion that vendors must cope with.

I hope this has set the stage for the speakers who are following me, and I sincerely hope they can answer these seemingly endless questions; questions which continue to evolve as yet another new system or service comes our way. As Macbeth views the apparitions which the witches conjured up, he says "whatever thou art, for thy good caution, thanks: thou hast harped my fear alright."[8] Call it confusion or call it fear, something is in the air.

REFERENCES

1. William Shakespeare, *Macbeth,* ed. by Kenneth Muir (The Arden Shakespeare), 8th ed., Cambridge: Harvard University Press, 1953, p. 109.
2. Ibid., p. 109.
3. Ibid., p. 109.
4. Ibid., p. 109.
5. Ronald G. Leach, "Electronic Document Delivery: New Options for Libraries," *Journal of Academic Librarianship,* 18 (6) (1993), p. 364.
6. Peggy Johnson, "When Pigs Fly, or When Access Equals Ownership," *Technicalities,* 12 (2) (February, 1992), p. 6.
7. John Cox, "The Changing Role of the Subscription Agent," *Interlending and Document Supply,* 20 (3) (1992), p. 109.
8. William Shakespeare, op. cit., p. 114.

BIBLIOGRAPHY

Cox, John. "The Changing Role of the Subscription Agent." *Interlending and Document Supply* 20 (3) (1992), pp. 108-110.
Johnson, Peggy. "When Pigs Fly, or When Access Equals Ownership." *Technicalities* 12 (2) (February, 1992), pp. 4-7.
Leach, Ronald G. "Electronic Document Delivery: New Options for Libraries." *Journal of Academic Librarianship* 18 (6) (1993), pp. 359-364.
Shakespeare, William. *Macbeth,* ed. by Kenneth Muir (The Arden Shakespeare). 8th ed. Cambridge: Harvard University Press, 1953.

Changing Relationships
in the Acquisition and Delivery
of Library Materials:
A Survey

Joyce L. Ogburn

SUMMARY. This paper reports on the results of a survey conducted in the summer of 1993 that was designed to determine the present state of and recent changes in relationships among librarians, vendors, publishers, and systems vendors. It also sought to understand whether the advent of document delivery to libraries was affecting services being offered by vendors.

In recent times I had been hearing both from librarians and materials vendors that their roles and relationships were getting muddled with all the new services and products being offered by vendors. Apparently relationships, roles, cooperation, and pricing models were changing. For example, as vendors and publishers have expanded their traditional services, they do not know whom to approach at the library regarding their new services. Also, acquisitions and serials librarians are confused about how the new services will affect traditional services and if they will no longer be involved in vendor selection for the library. Additionally, libraries' organizations, budgets, and responsibilities are changing, with the result that

Joyce L. Ogburn is Chief Acquisitions Librarian at Yale University, P. O. Box 1603A, Yale Station, New Haven, CT 06520.

[Haworth co-indexing entry note]: "Changing Relationships in the Acquisition and Delivery of Library Materials: A Survey." Ogburn, Joyce L. Co-published simultaneously in *Collection Management* (The Haworth Press, Inc.) Vol. 19, Nos. 3/4, 1995, pp. 11-27; and: *Practical Issues in Collection Development and Collection Access: The 1993 Charleston Conference* (ed: Katina Strauch et al.) The Haworth Press, Inc., 1995, pp. 11-27. Multiple copies of this article/chapter may be purchased from The Haworth Document Delivery Center [1-800-3-HAWORTH; 9:00 a.m. - 5:00 p.m. (EST)].

© 1995 by The Haworth Press, Inc. All rights reserved.
11

the publishers and vendors can not keep up with the priorities and contacts in the library. And to add one more element, everyone is asking more from the systems developers and expecting them to cooperate in acquiring, accessing and delivering information to library clientele.

A survey was written to determine whether and how these relationships had changed. The survey was prefaced as follows:

> In preparation for a discussion at the Charleston Conference, I am asking librarians, vendors, publishers, and systems vendors who read *Against the Grain* to answer a survey about how services and products that support information delivery and dissemination are developed and change over time. For example, document delivery (delivery for free or fee of articles or other publications to a library or to a requester) is a service being offered by more and more suppliers. With the apparently increasing need for this service the question, how the development of this service has affected other traditional roles or services among the four players, may be asked. Moreover, the question arises whether there is increasing overlap in the services being offered directly to information seekers.

The survey was kept short to encourage responses. But as a consequence, not many detailed questions could be asked. It was hoped that there would be enough responses to see some kind of trend in the answers. I did not specify one person per institution/place/business, but some respondents told me that someone with more authority would have to answer for their company or institution.

The survey was originally distributed in the June 1993 issue of the journal *Against the Grain*. The existence of the survey and a request for responses was advertised on Acqnet and the Collection Development electronic list. As a result of the electronic ads, there were requests for electronic copies, especially if the reader did not have a copy of the issue of *Against the Grain*.

RESULTS

Responses listed throughout are coded to indicate the number of responses by librarians (L), vendors (V), publishers (P), and systems vendors (S). First to be reported are the number of responses received and the mode of return to the author:

31L; 7V; 4P; 1S   total (43)
3L; 2V; 1P   electronic (6)
28L; 3P; 1S   mail (32)
7L; 1V; 1P   photocopy (9)
1L; 2V   fax (3)
21L; 2V; 2P; 1S original (26)

The number of responses was extremely small. *Against the Grain* has a circulation of approximately 2,000 and some responses were gained as a result of the advertising on electronic lists. I conclude that the results are not generalizable; however, the answers are offered here for whatever value they may be to the user.

General Results

As with all surveys, there are problems with interpretation by the respondents. One vendor filled out parts of the publisher and systems sections in addition to the vendor section. The one systems respondent only sent one page, so there is almost no data to report. Vendors, publishers and systems vendors were asked to rank how they determine priorities, but only 4 vendors and 2 publishers actually ranked their choices, whereas the others merely checked them off. Section VI in the questions about working with other players, vendors and publishers filled out all parts; librarians in general did not understand the question and either answered under just librarian, or all the others and not librarian. A few librarians indicated that they were totally baffled by this section and did not know how to respond.

Document Delivery

Three of seven vendors indicated that they offer document delivery services. There is no typical profile of a vendor who does:

1   offered almost all of the services listed and was international; main clientele was academic;

usually approached acquisitions/serials librarian, collection
development, or head of tech services;
for document delivery they went to serials librarian; and
pricing was offered unbundled or as one package
3   primarily sold electronic formats, international, only supplied
materials;
main clientele was academic, corporate and medical;
usually approached library director to offer new services and
document delivery; and
pricing was a combination of unbundled and in combination,
and the document delivery price was tied to other services
7   primarily offered serials, were international, and supplied
materials and a check-in system;
main clientele was academic, federal, corporate;
who they approached depended on the product: for document
delivery approached director, head of public service, or head
of access services; and
pricing was offered as both separate and in combination.

Although no clear profile emerged, all vendors had similar reasons why they began document delivery:

1   increasing diversion of serial resources,
3   cancellation of serials,
7   decline in subscriptions in favor of just-in-time delivery.

Profile in cooperation was as follows:

1   library more than 10, other vendor not indicated, publisher not
indicated, systems not indicated,
3   library more than 10, other vendor 1-5, publisher more than
10, systems more than 10,
7   library more than 10, other vendor more than 10, publisher
more than 10, systems more than 10.

Cooperative enhancements included:

1   library EDI and document delivery, other vendor no indication, publisher EDI and document delivery, systems EDI;

3 library EDI and document delivery, other vendor no indication, publisher EDI and document delivery, systems no indication;

7 library EDI, other vendor EDI, publisher EDI, systems EDI .

Their individual views of the other players were:

1 library partner, other vendor competitor, publisher combination, systems partner;

3 library partner, other vendor combination, publisher partner, systems combination;

7 library partner, other vendor combination, publisher partner, systems partner.

As for believing whether relationships had changed in the last 5 years:

1 yes,
3 yes,
7 no.

Librarians

There were two librarians who indicated that they would be primary decision makers if offered new products or services. They profiled as follows:

14 monographs, serials, acquisitions, and collection development;

17 monographs, serials, acquisitions, collection development, automation, and management.

Those involved in decision to choose a vendor for document delivery showed no pattern of common responsibilities:

8 monographs, serials, acquisitions, and collection development;

11 monographs, serials, acquisitions, and collection development, newspapers, microforms, and government documents;

16 acquisitions and collection development;

20 monographs, serials, and acquisitions;

23   monographs, serials, and acquisitions.

Also nothing emerged from looking at their profile of cooperation, since this section was left incomplete by many librarians. All
were among those who said relationship had changed in 5 years.

The next section provides the actual survey results.[1] A conclud-
ing paragraph follows these results.

SURVEY RESULTS

I. Librarian

Library characteristics:

A Type
   26   Academic
   1   Public
   0   Corporate
   3   Medical
   0   Law
   1   Other: Government

B Automated system
   29   Yes 1 Developed in-house   24 Purchased
   2   No

Your primary responsibility (check all that apply):

A 23   Monographs
   21   Serials

B 27   Acquisitions
   12   Collection Development
   12   Other: 3 government documents
                    2 automation
                    1 cataloging
                    1 copy cataloging
                    1 reference

1 newspapers
1 microforms
1 management
1 binding and marking

Services or products of materials vendors presently used:

29 Supply of library materials
3   Authorities work
3   Recon
9   Cataloging records
9   Document delivery
9   Serials check in system
11 Acquisitions system
2   Other: 1 electronic ordering
               1 management reports, electronic ordering

New services or products you would like them to offer:

1   needs A/V supplier for curriculum resources collection

If materials vendors were to be used by your library other than for supply of materials, your role in the decision process would be:

2   Primary decision maker
14   Participant in decision
0   No participation
2   Not sure
15   Depends on the service or product

If your library is using a materials vendor, publisher, or systems vendor for document delivery, were you involved in the choice of vendor (circle the category of supplier)?

10   N/A
5   Yes
10   No

Has the choice of supplier for document delivery affected your use of materials vendors?

0   Yes
19   No

II. Materials Vendor

Major concentration (check all that apply)

A 4   Monographs
  3   Serials
  2   Electronic formats
  2   Other: 1 A/V
               1 continuations/standing orders

B 3   Domestic
  3   Foreign
  4   International

Services or products offered (check all that apply):

7   Supply of library materials
2   Authorities work
2   Recon
2   Cataloging records
3   Document delivery
2   Serials check in system
1   Acquisitions system
4   Other: 1 public services, TOC
              1 A/V
              1 data bases, TOC, reports, bibliographies
              1 physical processing

Services or products planned:

1   interlinking stand alone system with other systems

Primary library market (check all that apply):

6   Academic
2   Public

3   Corporate
2   Medical
1   Law
3   Other: 1 school
         1 sci/tech
         1 federal

III. Systems Vendors

Primary library market (check all that apply):

1S   Academic
1S   Public
1S   Corporate
1S   Medical
1S   Law
0S   Other

Functions supported in your system (check all that apply):

A 0V; 1S Acquisitions   1
  1V; 1S Serials check-in   2
  0V; 1S Circulation   1
  0V; 1S ILL   1
  0V; 1S Cataloging   1
  0V; 1S Collection Development   1
  0V; 1S OPAC   1
  0V; 1S Citation databases   1
  0V; 1S Patron requests   1
  1V; 1S Document delivery   2
  1V; 1S   Other: 1V TOC
                      1S Z39.50, etc.

B 1S   Integrated
  1S   Turn key

Services or products planned:

1S   voice response system (via phone) for circulation, materials
      booking

IV. Publisher

Sales to libraries:

A Percentage of total sales:
1   30%
1   80%
1   85%
1   90%

B Primary library market (check all that apply):
4   Academic
2   Public
4   Corporate
4   Medical
3   Law
1   Other: 1 government

Primary area of publishing:

3   Monographs
2   Serials
3   Electronic publications
1   Microformats
2   Other: 1 multivolume series
1 electronic databases

What electronic developments have you implemented:

1V; 3P Bar codes on product   4
1V; 3P EDI with buyers   4
1V; 3P EDI with other publishers   4
0V; 3P Online database/inventory   3
1V; 4P Email (external)   5

V. Materials Vendors, Systems Vendors, and Publishers

When offering new services or products, the person first approached at the library is:

3V; 2P Acquisitions/serials librarian 5
3V; 2P Collection development librarian 5
0V; 0P Systems librarian 0
3V; 0P Head of Technical Services 3
2V; 2P Library director 4
0V; 1P Other: 1P subject specialist 1
4V; 2P Depends on the service or product 6

If you offer document delivery services, whom did you first approach in the library to offer this service?

1V serials
1V director;
1V N/A
1V director, head public services, head access services

1P library director for pilot study
1P N/A

If you offer a document delivery service, what major factor influenced the decision to implement this service?

1V increasing diversion of serials resources
1V cancellation of serials
1V decline in subscriptions in favor of just-in-time
1V N/A

1P serials cancellations
1P N/A

Do you offer document delivery directly to end users?

3V; 0P Yes 3
1V; 3P No 4
1V; 0P N/A 1

If you do not support document delivery, have you lost library accounts to a vendor who does?

0V; 0P Yes 0
2V; 2P No 4

0V; 1P Don't know   1
1V; 1P N/A   2

Pricing for all services or products are offered:

A 3V; 1P Unbundled   4
  0V; 1P As one package   1
  3V; 1P Combination of the two   4
  1V; 0P N/A   1

B If services or products are priced separately, do you plan to offer them as a package?

3V; 2P Yes 5
1V; 0P No   1
0V; 1P N/A 1

C Do you tie the price of use of document delivery services to other services?

2V; 1P Yes 3
1V; 1P No   2
0V; 1P N/A 1

Please rank your means for determining priorities for new services or products:

5V; 4P User surveys   9
6V; 4P Discussions with largest clients   10
4V; 3P User meetings   7
0V; 2P User advisory council   2
2V; 3P Meetings with materials vendors   5
3V; 3P Meetings with systems vendors   6
2V; 3P Meetings with publishers   5

VI. All

Interaction with clients/vendors:

27L; 7V; 4P Paper   37

18L; 5V; 3P Online ordering and claiming 25
9L; 3V; 1P Search only online database 12
16L; 7V; 3P Internet   25
8L; 5V; 2P Dial in   17
19L; 6V; 3P Email   27
0L; 1V; 0P fax   1
0L; 1V; 0P telephone   1

How often have you worked with others to develop standards, systems, services, or new products?

Library:			Materials Vendor:		
8L; 0V; 0P	Never	8	3L; 0V; 0P	Never	3
13L; 0V; 0P	1-5x	12	3L; 2V; 0P	1-5x	5
2L; 1V; 0P	5-10x	3	1L; 1V; 0P	5-10x	2
4L; 4V; 3P	> 10x	11	1L; 3V; 2P	> 10x	6

Publisher:			Systems Vendor:		
6L; 0V; 0P	Never	6	3L; 0V; 0P	Never	3
0L; 0V; 1P	1-5x	2	3L; 1V; 0P	1-5x	4
0L; 2V; 0P	5-10x	2	0L; 1V; 0P	5-10x	1
0L; 2V; 2P	> 10x	4	1L; 2V; 3P	> 10x	6

At present with whom are you working to develop these enhancements?

Library:			Materials Vendor:		
2L; 5V; 1P	EDI	8	2L; 2V; 3P	EDI	7
6L; 2V; 3P	Doc del	1	1L; 1V; 2P	Doc del	4
16L; 0V; 0P	Nothing	15	6L; 0V; 0P	Nothing	6
0L; 1V; 1P	Other:		0L; 0V; 1P	Other:	
1P	New product		1P New product		
1V	SISAC, ICEDIS, X12				

Publisher:			Systems Vendor:		
0L; 6V; 2P	EDI	9	2L; 5V; 2P	EDI	9

1L; 2V; 1P   Doc del 4   0L; 0V; 2P   Doc del 2
6L; 0V; 0P   Nothing 6   6L; 0V; 0P   Nothing 6
0L; 0V; 1P   Other:
    1P new product

In the delivery and dissemination of information you view the following as:

Library: Materials Vendor:

16L; 7V; 4P   Partner 27   14L; 0V; 2P   Partner 16
0L; 0V; 0P   Compet. 0   1L; 3V; 0P   Compet. 4
5L; 0V; 0P   Combin. 5   2L; 4V; 1P   Combin. 7

Publisher: Systems Vendor:

11L; 6V; 1P   Partner 18   13L; 6V; 1P   Partner 20
0L; 2V; 3P   Compet. 6   0L; 0V; 0P   Compet. 1
5L; 0V; 1P   Combin. 6   4L; 1V; 3P   Combin. 8

VII. Comments

In your opinion, has the relationship among these four players changed in the last five years?

25L; 4V; 3P Yes   32
1L; 3V; 0P   No   4
1L; 0V; 0P   Don't know   1

If yes, how?

A REPRESENTATIVE SAMPLE OF ALL THE RESPONSES

Librarians

". . . Now, publishers and vendors are focusing on the delivery and dissemination of information as a new opportunity as the number of books and subscriptions purchased by libraries declines."

"Public service areas . . . are getting 'acquainted' with traditionally tech services materials vendors–whole new world."

"Closer collaboration for some areas (standards, EDI) more competition in struggle to define roles."

". . . Problems in relationship between libraries and publishers over issues such as copyright (e.g., Texaco case) are being brought to the forefront and have no easy solution."

"Materials vendors are moving into document delivery relationship with publishers. Libraries have more choices. Many journal publishers will move from paper to electronic delivery; big impact on systems."

". . . Libraries are helping to shape the products and services they need . . ."

". . . My involvement/knowledge of systems has increased over the years."

". . . I think there is also some competition among these 4 that didn't exist before, as vendors/publishers begin to identify potential sources for new materials in an information- and service-driven society."

"As staffs have decreased vendors are seen as an alternative to 'doing it ourselves . . .' "

"Systems vendors have a lot of competition. RFPs are very exacting and Libraries believe the systems people will come through with what Libraries want. I think this is an area where we end up compromising more than planned but it is lot better than the old days of local system development."

"The major change is . . . who is the partner and who the competitor . . ."

Vendors

"Increasing cooperation within both libraries and library system providers for tech services cost reduction."

"More competitors in doc del/TOC all vying for the same shrinking dollars."

"New technology has changed the way we interact with our customers and publishers . . ."

"No–still woefully inadequate, though vendor library interactions have improved."

Publishers

"A great deal of cooperation among vendors/publishers to electronically streamline costs and processes . . ."

"It's much more interdependent."

"Publishers have become much more aware of the changing markets and have begun to realize that there are opportunities to replace turnover lost due to cancellations. In an electronic future, agents and other vendors become obsolete, if direct delivery to individuals becomes a reality, serials librarians themselves may become obsolete. There is nothing like threats and opportunities to bring the players together to forge new alliances. Publishers see libraries as natural allies but the feeling is not altogether mutual at the moment."

ADDITIONAL COMMENTS

Librarian

"We are working out new relationships within the library slowly at the same time that vendors and publishers are developing new relationships. ILL is still very separate from acquisitions and some of us are trying to redefine the relationship, particularly in relation to journal subscriptions, formal articles, and library support of these resources . . ."

"Many more issues surrounding licensing and copyright permissions."

"I've heard that doc delivery is an area libraries should be investigating as a possible money maker. We have the collections and the ILL expertise. We shouldn't let others do what we could do (and pay them to do besides)."

". . . Is the librarian necessary?"

Publisher

". . . The gulf between the big players and the small is widening as the latter do not have time, expertise and money to devote to development. There is a real distinction between electronic options for the primary and secondary publishers . . ."

CONCLUSIONS

Although the number of survey responses was small, they do seem to indicate that relationships and services are changing, but it is probably too soon to know what the effects of document delivery are going to be on competition, services, pricing, choice of vendor, or vendor relations with the library. The survey may not have asked enough to determine how libraries are viewing publishers and publisher services, or whether publishers will continue to see libraries as being such a large proportion of their market. It may also be too soon to know how systems vendors are going to fit into the picture for the library, although they are key to effectively implementing such developments as EDI.

NOTE

1. Copies of the survey were also distributed at the Charleston Conference in November 1993, with the intention of gathering more responses. Only a few responses were returned, and those results are not included in this paper.

The Case for Acquiring and Accessing Electronic Journals in Libraries

Nancy Markle Stanley

SUMMARY. This paper provides arguments why libraries should make available both free and fee-based electronic serials and why it is imperative that they move quickly. It features discussions of the costs of acquiring and storing materials, customer services, and the future of libraries. Incorporated are strategies for assuring that libraries will continue to play an important role in the distribution of information into the next millennium.

INTRODUCTION

Many libraries have begun to access and acquire electronic journals because it is an extension of what libraries have always done, i.e., acquire information in all forms. Electronic-based information, however, is not simply another new form, but perhaps the most important source of information developed this century. The historical significance of electronic publishing is akin to that of the printed book and will have profound effects on every facet of the future for librarians, vendors of information, and information gatherers everywhere. Just as television never replaced radio, electronic serials will

Nancy M. Stanley is a member of the Acquisitions Management Team at The Pennsylvania State University Libraries, E506 Pattee Library, University Park, PA 16802.

[Haworth co-indexing entry note]: "The Case for Acquiring and Accessing Electronic Journals in Libraries." Stanley, Nancy Markle. Co-published simultaneously in *Collection Management* (The Haworth Press, Inc.) Vol. 19, Nos. 3/4, 1995, pp. 29-34; and: *Practical Issues in Collection Development and Collection Access: The 1993 Charleston Conference* (ed: Katina Strauch et al.) The Haworth Press, Inc., 1995, pp. 29-34. Multiple copies of this article/chapter may be purchased from The Haworth Document Delivery Center [1-800-3-HAWORTH; 9:00 a.m. - 5:00 p.m. (EST)].

© 1995 by The Haworth Press, Inc. All rights reserved.
29

not entirely supplant print versions.[1] However, this revolution will markedly impact the format in which information will be made available in the future, and who will provide user access.

COSTS

In these days of shrinking budgets, the special role of collection development and acquisitions librarians is to acquire high quality information for the best price and to spend reduced budgets in the most efficient and effective manner possible. Electronic journals hold the potential for helping to lower the costs of acquiring library materials.[2] If production costs were the primary consideration, subscription dollars for electronic serials would be less than for comparable print versions, reduced perhaps by as much as ten to forty percent. This would depend on whether commercial publishers, university presses, or libraries publish them. Commercial publishers expect, of course, to reap profits similar to those currently derived from the sale of print journals. In a networked environment, libraries should be able to reduce their commitment of budget dollars to the acquisitions of printed materials by relying instead on electronic access. In the future, libraries will most likely be able to meet most user needs by negotiating site licenses, providing pay-per-use alternatives, and/or by exploring some combination of services that will assure that material costs and delivery needs are met.

There are other ways that digitized information is already reducing library costs. Electronic serials are far less expensive to store than print journals. There is no contest when comparing the current and future costs of providing physical facilities with the cost of computer storage and this scenario is unlikely to change. With technological advances, computer memory will continually become less and less expensive. Conversely, the costs for maintaining physical facilities for print materials will likely take quantum leaps. In addition, it will be less expensive to process and distribute information in the electronic environment, requiring in many instances only a few keystrokes to assure availability.

Perhaps the most compelling argument for acquiring electronic journals and other forms of digitized information is ecological, i.e., saving the trees and our environment. Preserving our natural resources for future generations has become one of the most critical issues of our times. Over time, as information gatherers learn to work in this new medium, they will print only what they need and recycle when finished with it, depending on computer-based archiving for storage.

CUSTOMER SERVICE

The desire to provide good customer service has always been a primary aim of librarians and, within the limits of past technologies and budgets, most libraries have provided the best possible services available. These days, however, patrons are much more demanding. In general, they are beginning to understand the relationship between computer technology and the information gathering opportunities that it provides. Accordingly, they have escalated their demands.

Library users constitute a very diverse group. They range from the casual reader to world class researchers. The challenge for librarians is to build a scholar-centered information universe that is readily available and supports and facilitates communication among scholars. Libraries are not only challenged, but also mandated to seek the best possible services for patrons in order to advance the knowledge of science and literature throughout the world.

CUSTOMERS DEMAND SPEEDY DELIVERY

A primary concern of patrons is the inability of libraries to deliver information in a timely manner. Steve Cisler admonishes librarians with this quote, "If I read in a journal [meaning print, of course], I am not in the loop–[a] computer scientist to a librarian."[3] We now spend approximately seventy percent of our materials budgets on printed serial literature. Historically, printed journals have been considered the speediest form of communication for scholars. Yet it generally takes several months from the beginning of the creative process to the end product. In the electronic environment, scholars are able to transmit the result of their work as quickly as it is completed and, furthermore, can receive feedback in an equally speedy manner. With the capability of electronic serials, many scholars can be much more productive over their lifetimes. It brings to mind, for example, how much more advanced cancer or AIDS research might be today if investigators had always been able to share their knowledge across the networks in the same timely fashion that is now available.

CUSTOMER TAILORED INFORMATION

Many library customers are also demanding that libraries provide services in the form of information packages that are tailored to individual needs. What's more, they want these delivered electronically to their office work stations! While this demand may appear to be a bit unreasonable, it really isn't. A whole new realm of interesting capabilities is available with digitized data. The nature of electronic text is such that it is dynamic, adaptable and "potentially eminently interactive."[4] Information in digitized form greatly reduces the limitations associated with the printed word.

There are a number of unique and powerful software tools available for searching and manipulating data. In fact, the possibilities of digitized information are nearly endless. It is, therefore, imperative that professionals involved in the information enterprise take advantage of these new features and ensure that customer needs are met.

THE FUTURE

Some say the future of libraries is at stake. The following quote appeared in a recent article of *Newsweek*: "Today information is the wellspring of great fortunes, much as land was a century ago. . . . [It] can race along electronic 'superhighways' at the speed of light. After years of hype about what the 'digital future' would look like, the future has started to arrive, heralded (as it always is) by an unmistakable sound: that of money hitting the table."[5] If it is being addressed in the popular literature, it may already be too late. There should be no mistake that librarians and anyone else involved in the business of distributing information must embrace electronic sources and do it quickly. Without a doubt, information professionals are confronted with competitors who have clout, the likes of which they have never seen before. What has always been the bailiwick of librarians, the collection and distribution of information, has become the target of considerable corporate interest–interest that is quite capable, if you will, of hitting the table with the awesome sound of money.

Rather than view new corporate interest as competition, it is imperative that librarians see the electronic revolution as an opportunity and join forces to let the corporate enterprises know what they have to offer the electronic revolution. They need to explore and carve out a position in this new age. The challenge for libraries and librarians is to change and to change rapidly. The question is how and in what direction.

SOME STRATEGIES FOR LIBRARIES AND LIBRARIANS

Librarians and their staffs need to embrace change by seeking and becoming experts in the characteristics and uses of computerized information and data. They need to develop a detailed understanding of the business of producing, distributing, and storing information both in print and electronic forms and make knowledge-based comparisons. Librarians need to become more actively involved in seeking solutions to some very serious issues associated with digitized information. While issues in the electronic environment (e.g., assuring access for all users, preservation, and guaranteeing intellectual property rights) are clearly in the process of being resolved, librarians need to provide input at every front, take a stand, and demonstrate support for proposed solutions.

Librarians must positively confront these challenging new times. It is important to assume leadership on behalf of our organizations and within our organizations, acting as a model for staff. Massive technology training for all staff needs to be provided. Staff members should be encouraged to be creative and empowered to do all that they can to advance the cause of our customers and libraries.

Library organizations must also seek cooperative opportunities for sharing electronic information across institutions and the networks. Librarians need to network themselves, their ideas, and resources to a degree unheard of in the past. What has long been thought of as something belonging to some distant future has clearly arrived and is here to stay. Electronic information is as revolutionary as radio, television, or even the printed word. The only choice left to professionals involved in the information enterprise is to embrace and take advantage of it.

NOTES

1. Metz, Paul and Paul M. Gherman. "Serial Pricing and the Role of the Electronic Journal," *College & Research Libraries*, 52 (4) (July 1991): 322.
2. Ibid, 322.
3. Cisler, Steve. "Convergent Electronic Cultures," *Serials Review*, 18 (1-2): 55.
4. HEIRAlliance. "What Presidents Need to Know . . . About the Future of University Libraries: Technology and Scholarly Communications," *HEIRAlliance Executive Strategies Report*, 2 (June 1993): 2.
5. "Eyes On the Future and Big Money On the Table." *Newsweek* (May 31, 1993): 39.

Negotiating for Electronic Journal Indexes

Randy J. Olsen

INTRODUCTION

During the 1992/93 fiscal year, Brigham Young University (BYU) engaged in two important collection development initiatives. First, BYU undertook a vendor evaluation project designed to either reaffirm existing business relationships with its approval, firm order, and continuations vendors or to transfer those acquisition programs to one or more new vendors. The second initiative was to identify and provide access to selected electronic journal indexing services that could best satisfy student and faculty research needs. This second project was pursued concurrently with a similar effort by the Utah College Library Council (UCLC) to provide statewide access to electronic journal indexes.

In this paper I will briefly contrast the objectives of the vendor evaluation and database selection projects at BYU, compare the decision making processes associated with both, and make some observations about the perspective and negotiating skills required of collection development personnel in dealing with book vendors as opposed to database suppliers. I will also review the objectives of the UCLC project and comment on the importance of cooperative ventures to the future of library support for higher education. Finally,

Randy J. Olsen is Deputy University Librarian at Brigham Young University, 3080 HBLL, Provo, UT 84602.

[Haworth co-indexing entry note]: "Negotiating for Electronic Journal Indexes." Olsen, Randy J. Co-published simultaneously in *Collection Management* (The Haworth Press, Inc.) Vol. 19, Nos. 3/4, 1995, pp. 35-45; and: *Practical Issues in Collection Development and Collection Access: The 1993 Charleston Conference* (ed: Katina Strauch et al.) The Haworth Press, Inc., 1995, pp. 35-45. Multiple copies of this article/chapter may be purchased from The Haworth Document Delivery Center [1-800-3-HAWORTH; 9:00 a.m. - 5:00 p.m. (EST)].

© 1995 by The Haworth Press, Inc. All rights reserved.

I will detail the some of the decisions made by BYU and UCLC on electronic journal indexing services.

BYU PROJECT OBJECTIVES AND DECISION MAKING PROCESS

BYU launched its vendor evaluation project primarily because the library had not compared its vendors against their competitors in nearly twenty years. While the library was not particularly dissatisfied with the services and discounts currently in place, neither were we certain that they were the best available to our university. We also believed that it might be possible to reduce some personnel costs associated with collection development and acquisitions by preferring vendors with automated systems that would interface well with our acquisitions module and operating procedures.

The Vendor Evaluation Project was conducted by a small Task Force of the Lee Library's Collection Management and Development Committee. This Task Force developed a request for proposal, evaluated proposals received from five vendors, conducted over fifty hours of telephone interviews with vendor references, and hosted vendor on-site visits. Interaction between the Task Force and vendors was characterized by open, honest dialogue, with both sides anxious to share information about the costs and benefits of establishing a business relationship. The final vendor selections were made by the Task Force and reported to the Collection Management and Development Committee.

By contrast, the selection of electronic indexing services for BYU was a much less formalized and much more consultative endeavor. General consensus on the need to expand electronic reference services beyond CD ROM indexes grew out of numerous discussions in the library's Reference Services Committee and the Integrated Library Systems Committee. Selection of databases to be evaluated came from those same two committees, but was also heavily influenced by input from teaching faculty and by discussions in the Utah College Library Council on providing indexing services across the state network. Final decisions on which electronic services to contract for were made by the Reference Services Committee only after extensive consultation with all of the other groups. The Collection Management and Development Committee was not heavily involved in the process, even though funding for the indexes came from the collection development funding.

PROCESS REFLECTS PARADIGM SHIFT

The vendor evaluation and electronic indexing projects at BYU can be viewed as two separate, unrelated collection development activities, and indeed they were conducted in that manner. They could also be seen, however, as movement within one library consistent with the much talked about paradigm shift from ownership to access. A primary objective of the vendor evaluation project was to reduce costs of collection building, while the electronic indexing initiative focused on expanding access to information, whether owned, leased, or remotely mounted. New costs associated with electronic access were accepted and, indeed, seen in some degree as compensatory expenditures for recent loss of journal subscriptions.

The decision making processes of the two projects were reflective of the differences in objectives. In the vendor evaluation effort, decisions were reached by a small group of experts in collection development and acquisitions based on negotiations with knowledgeable book vendors. Final vendor selections were based on each company's ability to meet expected discounts and known service demands.

Selection of electronic indexes were made only after hours of consultation among reference librarians, automation's personnel, and faculty. None of these players considered themselves experts in electronic services and all of them struggled to understand the financial, technical, and service ramifications of their decisions. Vendor representatives were scarcely more confident of their expertise. Sales representatives could negotiate pricing, but they lacked answers to technical questions; technical staff could respond to most questions about compatibility and connectivity, but wisely stayed out of pricing negotiations.

Based on BYU's experience with the vendor evaluation and electronic indexing projects and on my knowledge of recent collection development initiatives in other Utah academic libraries, I would like to offer the following observations:

1. Academic libraries in Utah, consciously or unconsciously, are taking concrete action moving them away from the ownership model and toward the access model of providing information.
2. Collection development decision making in this new environment will often require librarians to act not as experts, but as service providers seeking input from their customers. Decision making will be a consultative process involving many groups of interested parties. Reference librarians and other service personnel will play an increasingly important role.
3. Rapidly advancing technology will not permit vendors of electronic information to become masters of their business in the same sense as their colleagues in the book trade.
4. Decision making in the new environment will require collection development librarians to select from among alternatives for delivering information and each alternative will carry its own costs and benefits.

In the next section of this paper I will expand on this last observation by reviewing decisions reached by BYU and the Utah College Library Council on electronic indexing services.

BYU's CONSIDERATION
OF ELECTRONIC INDEXING SERVICES

As noted earlier, initial recommendations at BYU on electronic indexing services were developed by the library's Reference Services Committee. This Committee sought first to identify databases that would provide broad subject coverage, and second, to select files that could be made available across the university network in faculty offices, student labs, and student dorms. Along with a selection of subject specific databases such as Biosis and PsycINFO, the Committee recommended acquiring either IAC's Expanded Academic Index and General Business File, UMI's Periodical Abstracts and ABI/Inform, or the Wilson family of indexes.

Because the library requested new database funding, the University Administration sponsored a survey of college deans to determine the depth of their support for library electronic indexing services. Deans were asked if they would be willing to commit a portion of their college's capital equipment funds to purchase library databases. Six out of twelve colleges supported the Wilson indexes. The university administration was sufficiently impressed with the library's argument for electronic services and with the college deans' support for the project to award $135,000 in new funding. While this level of new funding was generous, it would not support access to all of the databases under review.

UCLC CONSIDERATION OF ELECTRONIC FILES

At the same time BYU was evaluating new electronic services, the UCLC, a consortium of eleven academic libraries in Utah, was pursuing a similar project. In 1992, UCLC recognized several trends occurring in the state. First, the major academic libraries were continuing to cancel journal subscriptions because of rising prices. Second, those same institutions were planning to expand their electronic reference capabilities by either adding tape loaded journal indexes to their OPACs or by providing access to remotely mounted journals. And third, the university libraries in the state were initiating trials of commercial document delivery services to evaluate their potential to compensate for journal cancellations. UCLC's Collection Development Committee became convinced that these three initiatives should be pursued cooperatively and placed particular emphasis on selecting electronic indexing services to be shared statewide.

At the state level, the process for selecting electronic indexes was similar to that followed at BYU. Over the course of several months, members of UCLC's Collection Development Committee proposed those electronic indexing services that could best meet the needs of the largest number of students and faculty in the state. E-mail debate framed arguments for and against various services in preparation for meetings where final decisions were to be reached. In support of the decision making process, collection development officers at the University of Utah, Utah State University, and BYU negotiated consortium pricing on behalf of the UCLC membership.

Databases under consideration again included the IAC, UMI, and Wilson indexes plus ERIC, LEXIS/NEXIS, Periodical Contents, and

PsycINFO. As has generally been the case with all types of cooperative collection development endeavors, UCLC found it extraordinarily difficult to reach consensus. Opinion was divided on which of the IAC, UMI, and Wilson indexes could best serve the state, and on whether it would be preferable to mount those files locally or to access them through OCLC, RLG, or CARL.

In general, the smaller college libraries, all of whom had Dynix systems, were skeptical about the feasibility of providing effective service from indexes mounted at the universities. These colleges tended to favor a statewide OCLC contract. The universities were more enthusiastic about local files, but they were divided on which of the IAC, UMI, and Wilson indexes would best meet the needs of their students and faculty.

BYU's IAC, UMI, AND WILSON COVERAGE STUDY

BYU performed a laborious title by title comparison of journal coverage in the IAC, UMI, and Wilson databases to guide its own selection of a general indexing service and to inform UCLC's decision making process. Table 1 shows the outcome of this study. The comparison revealed that although there is tremendous overlap among the indexes there are also a significant number of titles covered uniquely by each of the three companies.

Expanding the title by title analysis to each of the individual IAC, UMI, and Wilson indexes suggested subject areas where overlap and unique coverage is greatest, as is shown in Table 2. This table indicates that while Wilson offers more unique coverage than IAC or UMI, Wilson's coverage is concentrated in only five of its indexes: Applied Science and Technology index, Art Index, Biological and Agricultural Index, Education Index, Index to Legal Periodicals, and Library Literature. The titles in Wilson's other six files are also covered almost entirely by IAC and UMI indexes.

It is difficult to say anything definitive about unique subject coverage in IAC's Expanded Academic Index and UMI's Periodical Abstracts. Examining their business files, however, shows how significant each of these indexes are. IAC's General Business File includes nearly 400 unique titles while almost 500 unique journals are indexed in UMI's ABI Inform.

TABLE 1. Brigham Young University, Harold B. Lee Library: Comparison of Journal Coverage in Wilson, IAC, and UMI Products

The following comparisons were taken from journal listings provided by Information Access Company, UMI, and H. W. Wilson during 1993. Statistics shown should be taken only as general indicators of unique and overlap coverage. There are, undoubtedly, some errors in the report caused by title changes recognized by one company but not by another, because there are minor differences in the ways some titles are listed by each company, and because each company periodically adds to and deletes titles from their indexes.

Indexing Service	Unique Coverage	IAC Wilson Overlap	UMI Wilson Overlap	IAC UMI Overlap	IAC UMI Wilson Overlap	Totals
IAC Expanded Academic and General Business File	479	128	- - -	516	1,308	2,431
UMI Periodical Abstracts and ABI/Inform	691	- - -	153	516	1,308	2,668
Wilson Indexes	1,660	128	153	- - -	1,308	3,249

TABLE 2. Comparison of Journal Coverage in Wilson, IAC, and UMI Products

Indexing Service	Unique Coverage	IAC Wilson Overlap	UMI Wilson Overlap	IAC UMI Overlap	IAC UMI Wilson Overlap	Totals
IAC Expanded Academic Index	88	80	- - -	269	1,061	1,498
IAC General Business File	391	50	- - -	273	372	1,086
Total	**479**	**130**	**- - -**	**542**	**1,433**	**2,584**
UMI Periodical Abstracts	203	- - -	107	287	1,083	1,680
UMI ABI/Inform Global	488	- - -	46	253	362	1,149
Total	**691**	**- - -**	**153**	**540**	**1,445**	**2,829**
Wilson Applied Science and Technology Index	220	87	12	- - -	72	391
Wilson Art Index	167	0	3	- - -	40	210
Wilson Biological and Agricultural Index	165	2	5	- - -	52	224
Wilson Book Review Digest	17	0	1	- - -	72	90
Wilson Business Abstracts	5	22	16	- - -	288	331
Wilson Education Index	304	2	15	- - -	77	398
Wilson General Science Index	15	1	4	- - -	116	136
Wilson Humanities Index	0	6	3	- - -	327	336
Wilson Index to Legal Periodicals	571	11	15	- - -	56	653
Wilson Library Literature	188	1	10	- - -	19	218
Wilson Readers' Guide	7	0	78	- - -	151	236
Wilson Social Sciences Index	1	4	0	- - -	337	342
Total	**1,660**	**136**	**162**	**- - -**	**1,607**	**3,565**

Titles covered by more than one index from the same company are included in counts. Total titles reported are, therefore, overstated.

The conclusions BYU reached from the IAC, UMI, Wilson comparison study were:

1. Access must be provided to Wilson's art, education, legal, library, and science indexes.
2. Access must be provided to either UMI's Periodical Abstracts and/or to the remainder of the Wilson indexes.
3. Access must be provided to both UMI's ABI/Inform and IAC's General Business File.

UCLC's RESPONSE TO THE STUDY AND FUNDING REQUEST

BYU's decisions on which indexes to make available to its students and faculty were not the only possible responses to the comparison study. Within the UCLC Collection Development Committee opinion remained divided on which databases could best serve undergraduates in all institutions. The University of Utah, for example, strongly advocated subscription to IAC files based on the favorable reaction of that school's students and librarians to IAC indexes on CD ROM.

Total consensus, in fact, was never achieved by UCLC during 1992, but a funding request for statewide database access was delivered to the Utah State Board of Regents, nevertheless. This request articulated the goals UCLC hoped to further by providing access to electronic services and enhanced document delivery. Those goals were:

1. To ensure that all Utah students and faculty, especially those now disadvantaged because of geographic location or inability to pay, will have access to information resources.
2. To broaden the range of materials available to Utah students and faculty beyond that which we can afford to own within the state.
3. To enable Utah's academic libraries to cut duplication of journals, redirect the savings to strengthen book collections, and cooperatively ensure the completeness of important journal holdings in the state.

Note that while these goals plainly convey the need to shift from ownership to access in Utah, they also make an important philosophical statement about the responsibility of academic libraries to higher education. This statement being that academic libraries are committed to ensure that all students and faculty in Utah, regardless of their institutional affiliation, will have access to the level of information services necessary to support their education and research.

In my opinion, this commitment would have made little practical sense in the past because Utah's academic libraries, like college and university libraries everywhere, were tied to the ownership model of providing service. BYU could not share the books and journals in its collection with students at Dixie College 300 miles away without disadvantaging BYU's own students. Print materials simply can not be used simultaneously by more than one individual. Neither were there any financial incentives to share resources in the past since publishers and vendors hardly discount books and journals for libraries that intend to make them available on interlibrary loan.

Under the access model of providing information, however, this statement could make both philosophical and practical sense. Electronic information can be made available simultaneously to multiple users in multiple locations and some providers of electronic information are willing to discount their resources to consortial groups. Each member library can then make available more information through its consortium than it could ever provide access to on its own and there would be no liability to individual members for sharing electronic information mounted at their institution. Experience in Utah last year validates this assumption about the benefits of a consortial approach to information access.

SUBSCRIPTION NEGOTIATIONS AND FUNDING

As a result of its 1992 funding request, UCLC was allocated $65,000 for electronic services while BYU had earlier received $135,000 for new databases. Neither allocation was adequate to acquire all of the information resources desired. Following the journal coverage study of IAC, UMI, and Wilson, the highest priority for both UCLC and BYU became providing access to the Wilson indexes. Proposals were sought from OCLC for statewide First-

Search access to Wilson files and from Wilson for a tape subscription to be mounted at Utah State University.

OCLC offered several options with differing simultaneous user capacity and with different subsets of the Wilson databases. While OCLC's proposals were significantly discounted for the consortium, the lowest option did not provide for an adequate number of simultaneous users, did not provide access to enough of the Wilson indexes, and was still thousands of dollars over UCLC's available funding.

Wilson's preliminary proposal provided unlimited searching of twelve indexes for all UCLC libraries. This service level would have certainly met Utah's projected needs, but the subscription cost was nearly $300,000, with BYU's fee alone totalling close to $50,000. Wilson's initial quote was then four times the funding available to UCLC, and would have required BYU to dedicate over one/third of its funding just to Wilson files.

Fortunately, negotiations with Wilson did not stop after this initial quote. Robert Murdoch, at Utah State, continued to discuss with Wilson alternatives for providing their files to all UCLC members. A package was finally agreed upon that would allow over 50 simultaneous users statewide for under $70,000.

BYU pursued negotiations with UMI and ultimately contracted for taped loads of Periodical Abstracts and ABI/Inform for $23,800 annually. Under this contract, other universities in Utah could access the UMI files at BYU for an annual fee of under $7,000 and the colleges in the state could use the databases for under $4,000. These costs were hardly more than each library would have paid for single user CD ROM workstations. Furthermore, UMI agreed to extend these terms to selected libraries outside of Utah including Idaho State University, Ricks College in Idaho, and BYU Hawaii.

Through exploring options for delivering electronic indexes and because of persistent negotiations for favorable pricing, UCLC was able to provide equal access in Utah for all students and faculty to one set of indexes. Although a major accomplishment, this was one comparatively small step toward a larger goal of equalizing access to all electronic information. UCLC remains committed to this larger effort and believes that the quality of higher education in Utah can be significantly enhanced if libraries continue to aggressively pursue the common interests of their students and faculty.

Vendor Evaluation

Lynne C. Branche Brown

PART ONE

According to the literature of Total Quality Management, the customer is always right and quality companies meet, or exceed, the customer's expectations. Penn State has been doing its version of TQM–which it calls "CQI–continuous quality improvement"– since 1992. Immersed in that for the last 18 months, I've been thinking about customer expectations and vendor performance, and I'd like to look at those two things for a little while this afternoon. How do we set performance standards? How do we measure performance, both our own performance and the performance of those whose customers we are (our vendors)?

Much of the time, evaluating vendors is something we do after we have an established relationship with a vendor. We look at our vendor's performance and ask, "What are we getting from our vendor?" Today I'd like to look at evaluating vendors from a different perspective–at the beginning–with "What do we hope we'll get from a vendor?" Another way of asking that question might be, "What do we expect from a vendor?" We'll begin by looking at what we expect from a vendor and how we develop expectations. I'll follow that with some methods for gathering data and analyzing vendor performance against those expectations.

Lynne C. Branche Brown is affiliated with Pennsylvania State University Libraries, E506 Pattee Library, University Park, PA 16802.

[Haworth co-indexing entry note]: "Vendor Evaluation." Brown, Lynne C. Branche. Co-published simultaneously in *Collection Management* (The Haworth Press, Inc.) Vol. 19, Nos. 3/4, 1995, pp. 47-56; and: *Practical Issues in Collection Development and Collection Access: The 1993 Charleston Conference* (ed: Katina Strauch et al.) The Haworth Press, Inc., 1995, pp. 47-56. Multiple copies of this article/chapter may be purchased from The Haworth Document Delivery Center [1-800-3-HAWORTH; 9:00 a.m. - 5:00 p.m. (EST)].

© 1995 by The Haworth Press, Inc. All rights reserved.

I think we all have a general sense of the kinds of things we expect, or set standards for, in relation to our vendors. A list of things that we have expectations about might include:

- price/discount
- delivery
  -fill rate
  -discrepancy rate
  -defect rate
- service attributes
  -location
  -mode of delivery
    efficiency
    reliability
    flexibility in lot sizing
  -frequency of contact
  -cooperative nature of the supplier
  -ability to respond to problems
  -parallel communications links
- technical attributes
  -enlightened management style
  -technical expertise
  -company wide philosophy 'do it right the first time'
- financial health

A quality vendor would strive to meet our expectations in these areas. How do we define our expectations? What is appropriate frequency of contact? No doubt each of us has certain local parameters that help define our expectations. How many of these parameters are unique to our own institution? How many do we share?

As the team leader for a quality improvement team in our department, I've been working with some of the tools of Total Quality Management. As we conducted customer interviews, I started wondering about customer expectations. There was a wide variety of expectations for serials processing among our various "customers." This led us to start talking about the customer service, both that which we give and that which our vendors provide.

In June of 1993, the eight supervisors in our acquisitions department began specifying what we expect of our vendors. The goal was to reach a common understanding of Penn State's expectations for vendor performance. Our expectations would be the standards that we would expect our vendors to meet. The expectations would also be the measuring stick for evaluating vendor performance.

Our expectations included:

A satisfactory fulfillment rate is:
- For domestic vendors: 85% of currently available (in print/in stock @ pub) within 90 days.
- For foreign vendors: 85% of currently available imprints within 150 days.

Satisfactory invoicing service is:
    Invoices that contain all required data, in the agreed upon format, 100% of the time.

Satisfactory customer service is:
A response to our query:
- For Rush orders: within 24 hours
- For non-rush orders: within 72 hours

Our other expectations included:
- Credibility: do what they say the can do
- Flexibility: follow instructions, especially special instructions in individual titles
- Technological currency: can receive fax transmissions and can provide ASCII files on request
- Honesty: provide clear, concise and accurate information on communications of all kinds
- Customer-based orientation

After we did this, I began wondering how these standards compared to standards set by other libraries. How many of you have standards for vendor performance that are this specific? How do yours compare with these? How many of you have told your vendors what your standards are? Are the "standards" we set for Penn State reasonable?

To help answer these questions, I perused the literature to find out how other "customers" set their expectations, how they decided what was reasonable, and how they applied the standards in evaluating vendor performance. One of the things that our CQI team found as it interviewed its customers was that some customers had very uninformed expectations. Without sufficient understanding of the parts of the process, they expected things we couldn't deliver. With education, we were able to negotiate more reasonable expectations. I wondered whether some of the expectations we'd listed for our vendors were equally unreasonable.

I began by looking for published standards for any kind of purchasing function, or performance of vendors. I found literature from a variety of different industries. While there is a wealth of information in the library literature about the importance of vendor performance, and the vendor/library relationship, I found only one specific reference to customer expectations–which said libraries expect 30% of an order filled within 30 days.[1] In the literature from the field of business logistics, operations, and purchasing, I found some interesting things about standards in general, and some about models for applying standards to performance.

One article cited different ways of arriving at standards for vendor performance, called absolute standards and internal company directed standards.[2] Absolute standards are sometimes also called "industry standards." One example of an industry standard comes from the area of customer service. An article on setting standards for quality service in logistics defined part of quality customer service as: "Telephone answering: pick up the phone on or before the third ring."[3]

Have we started to set standards for quality service in our industry? Do we have any 'absolute' standards for vendor performance in our industry?

Internal company directed standards are those standards set by you, your boss, or the boss's boss. These are the kinds of standards we were setting as we sat around a conference table and agreed on what we expected. I suspect that this is the type of standard we, as acquisitions librarians, most frequently apply as we evaluate the service our vendors provide.

Other articles described methods for setting standards which employ data gathering and analysis. These included competitive standards and "comparative across time" standards. The first of these establishes competitive standards. These are standards based on a comparison of two or more vendors, by judging them against each other. The second type compares a vendor's present performance to its past performance, thus being "comparative across time."[4]

Comparative standards and competitive standards are useful after you have an established relationship with a vendor. But the others, industry standards and internal company directed standards, can be set prior to establishing a relationship with a vendor. How does an industry arrive at an "absolute" standard? How did customer service people decide that quality phone answering is three rings, instead of two, or four? Did they ask customers how they felt if the phone wasn't answered within three rings? Did they evaluate customers' "irritation level" if the phone had rung more than three times?

Are our vendors asking us what we expect for fill rate or claim resolution? Which brings me to my second question–do our vendors know what we expect? Have they set expectations of their suppliers?

As I talked to one of our vendors about this, they showed me how they monitored their own performance–and how they were charting improvements to their performance. I asked if they had ever, as the customer of publishers, talked to their vendors, the publishers, about performance expectations. Did they have expectations–had they set performance standards–for the publishers.[5]

Similarly, I was talking recently to another vendor about performance. We had a concern about what was happening in the claiming cycle for items we didn't receive. They assured us that they were handling our account as a top priority. But as we talked, we discovered that what I, as the customer, really wanted to know was *how* they were doing what they did for us. That they were giving us top priority didn't help us much–if the process they were using was the problem. So lately, I've been wondering if maybe just telling each other what we expect–setting the standard–isn't enough.

To reiterate what we heard this morning, we all operate as part of a system. The ordering and receipt that the acquisitions department does is only one part of that system. The rest of the system rests with the vendor who provides services to us, and the publisher, who produces the materials needed by our patrons. How the acquisitions department does its job needs to be complemented by and coordinated with how our vendors do their part. What the vendor does needs to complement and coordinate with how publishers do their piece. We're all part of a "food chain" between the information needy (the patrons) and the information producers. So, the performance standards we set must incorporate all the pieces of the system, and must all work together to ultimately meet the needs of the final customer–the user of the material.

One of the things I read as I investigated this issue was titled "Strategic Supplier Partnering."[6] In the literature on just-in-time purchasing, strategic supplier relationships involve purchasing partners making a long term commitment to each other. Part of this commitment is the understanding that both parties will conform to the requirements of each other and work together to maximize processes for both of them.

As a small piece of a BIG system, is setting standards, and communicating them to our vendors enough? Do library vendors establish service policies that reflect average expectations of their customers? Do they try to meet the expectations of their biggest accounts? Again, do we have industry standards we all agree on?[7]

Should I quit worrying about whether Penn State's "standards" are reasonable? As I read the purchasing literature, I found that other purchasing entities had used a process much like the one we had used at Penn State for establishing our standards, called the nominal group process.[8] In the nominal group process each individual writes down their own opinion of their expectations for the vendor. The group then discusses what has been written down, with participants providing rationales for their expectations, if necessary. The group then arrives at consensus for standards. While it was comforting to know that the method we had used had a name, it still didn't tell me if our standards are similar to others' standards. I'm hoping that the discussion this afternoon will help answer that question.

PART TWO: METHODS FOR EVALUATING VENDORS

[This was not presented at the conference in the interest of time, but it is relevant to the topic and may be useful to those interested in vendor evaluation.]

I would like to shift gears and talk briefly about methods for evaluating the performance of the vendor against the standards that had been set. During my quest, I ran across some interesting ways of looking at how our vendors are doing at meeting standards.

Not surprisingly, there are two basic options: to be objective, or to be subjective. A particularly informative article in the *Journal of Purchasing and Materials Management* describes three different approaches, each having varying degrees of objectivity and subjectivity.[9]

The first, an example of a subjective method for evaluating vendors, is the "categorical approach to vendor evaluation." Each vendor's performance is categorized in specific areas, such as "cost," "speed," "accuracy." The categories are assigned performance ratings, such as "good," "average," "bad." This method is quick, and requires minimal data. However, it relies on the intuition, memory, and personal judgment of the evaluator, and is therefore the least precise (see Illustration 1).

A second, more objective approach, is the "cost-ratio method." This method uses standard cost analysis tools to evaluate vendor performance in terms of the cost of doing business with the vendor. This approach, heavy on number crunching, requires a detailed assessment of the total cost of each purchase, then an evaluation of the total cost to the value of the purchase (see Illustration 2). This "cost ratio" is then applied to arrive at a net adjusted cost of doing business with the vendor. In the illustration, I have broken down the

ILLUSTRATION 1. Categorical Vendor Evaluation.

Criteria	Vendor A	Vendor B	Vendor C
Discount	Good(+)	Avg	Avg
Response Time	Bad(−)	Good	Avg
Fullfilment Speed	Avg(0)	Good	Avg
Fullfilment Accuracy	Bad(−)	Good	Avg
Total	−1	+3	0

Supplier with the greatest total is supplying the greatest overall value.

ILLUSTRATION 2. Cost-Ratio Vendor Evaluation.

Criteria	Vendor A	Vendor B
Quality Costs		
Incoming Inspection	$25	$25
Error Correction	$100	$50
Returns/Rework	$100	$50
Total Quality Costs	$225	$175
Value of Purchase	$10,000	$10,000
Quality Cost Ratio	2.25%	1.75%
Delivery Cost Ratio	3%	2%
Discount/Service Charges	−3%	−3%
Total Penalty	2.25%	.75%
Net adjusted cost	$10,225.00	$10,075.00

Supplier with the lowest net adjusted cost is supplying the greatest overall value.

Quality Costs to arrive at a Quality Cost Ratio. This would be done for determining other cost ratios (such as Delivery Cost Ratio) as well. The break down for the others is not illustrated.

A third approach combines the qualitative elements of the categorical approach with the quantifiable procedures of the cost-ratio method. This approach is referred to as "linear averaging," or "the weighted point method" (see Illustration 3). In this method, evaluation factors, or criteria, are selected. Each criterion is assigned a numerical rating (a weight) which is representative of its importance to the whole. After weights are assigned, a scale of performance is assigned and ratings are assigned to each vendor for each area being evaluated. The ratings and weights are then calculated to arrive at a "value index" for each supplier. In this method, the weights assigned to the criteria are intuitive to the evaluators, but the ratings assigned are based on gathered data, thus lending some objectivity to the evaluation.

ILLUSTRATION 3. Linear Averaging Vendor Evaluation.

Criteria	Weight	Vendor A	Vendor B	Vendor C
Costs				
Quality Costs	.1	2	5	3
Discount	.3	4	4	5
Delivery Costs	.15	2	3	3
Service				
Fulfillment Speed	.05	3	5	2
Response Time	.05	1	5	3
Accuracy	.25	2	4	1
Value Index	1.0	2.4	3.65	2.75

Supplier with the highest index is supplying greatest overall value.

NOTES

1. Alessi, Dana, "Vendor Selection, Vendor Collection, or Vendor Defection," *Journal of Library Administration*, v. 16, no. 3, 1992, p. 123.

2. Henry, Gary T. et al., "Establishing Benchmarks for Outcome Indicators," *Evaluation Review*, v. 16, n. 2, 1992, pp. 131-150.

3. Lancioni, Richard, and John L. Gattorna, "Setting Standards for Quality Service in Logistics," *International Journal of Physical Distribution and Logistics*, v. 22, n. 2, 1992, p. 25.

4. Op. cit., p. 133.

5. At the conference one attendee pointed out that frequently vendors are dealing with sole source suppliers–that book they want is only available from that publisher. If they want the product, they must be willing to buy on the publisher's terms. Having a sole source for a product limits any customer in any attempt to set performance expectations.

6. Henrick, Thomas E., and Lisa M. Ellram, *Strategic Supplier Partnering: An International Study*, Tempe, Arizona: Arizona State University Research Park, Center for Advanced Purchasing Studies, 1993.

7. A conference attendee referred the group to ISO 9002 as a potential industry standard. The ISO 9000 series of standards provides quality guidelines for suppliers and procurers. In complying with ISO 9002, a supplier agrees to have systems in place which assure products that conform to specified requirements. It does not, however, set particular expectations. ISO 9004 provides a model for developing a

quality management system. See *ISO Quality Standards Collection, A Global Compilation*, Irvine, CA: Global Engineering Documents, 1991.

8. Harrington, Thomas C. et al., "A Methodology for Measuring Vendor Performance," *Journal of Business Logistics*, v. 12, n. 1, 1991, pp. 83-103.

9. Timmerman, Ed, "An Approach to Vendor Performance Evaluation," *Journal of Purchasing and Materials Management*, Winter 1986, pp. 2-8.

How Much Is Enough?
Establishing a Corridor of Adequacy
in Library Acquisitions

John S. Clouston

First and foremost, I'd like to say thank you to the conference organizers for inviting me to give a paper at the Charleston Conference this year. I've been attending this conference more or less regularly for some time, but this is the first time I've found myself on this side of the podium.

Whenever I think about library acquisitions budgets these days, I'm reminded of an anecdote told by an uncle of mine who was a Presbyterian minister in Belfast, Northern Ireland. In his Sunday school class was a bright, vivacious girl called Suzy, who would rather be socializing and playing than studying her catechism. When my uncle asked her how she was coming along, not expecting news of great progress, a rather sheepish Suzy replied: "Aye, weel, now, Reverend Clouston, I hae finished wi' Hope, but I've nae touched Redemption!" I think a lot of us can relate to Suzy's bleak predicament.

The idea for this paper grew out of my experience as Coordinator for Collections Management at The University of Western Ontario Library System. Western is probably not atypical in terms

John S. Clouston is Chief Librarian at King's College, the University of Western Ontario, London, Ontario, Canada N6A 2M3.

[Haworth co-indexing entry note]: "How Much Is Enough? Establishing a Corridor of Adequacy in Library Acquisitions." Clouston, John S. Co-published simultaneously in *Collection Management* (The Haworth Press, Inc.) Vol. 19, Nos. 3/4, 1995, pp. 57-75; and: *Practical Issues in Collection Development and Collection Access: The 1993 Charleston Conference* (ed: Katina Strauch et al.) The Haworth Press, Inc., 1995, pp. 57-75. Multiple copies of this article/chapter may be purchased from The Haworth Document Delivery Center [1-800-3-HAWORTH; 9:00 a.m. - 5:00 p.m. (EST)].

© 1995 by The Haworth Press, Inc. All rights reserved.

57

of academic libraries–roughly 20,000 students, 8 libraries (2 main and 6 other libraries, one of them a compact-storage low use facility), and an annual acquisitions budget in the neighborhood of $5.5 million.

Our *first* problem was that in the eyes of the University administration, the Library seemed to represent a great, black hole. There were dark mutterings that no matter how many millions were poured into library acquisitions, more was always needed.

A *second* problem was the instability of the Canadian dollar, which during my tenure of 5 years as Coordinator: Collections Management, had been at various times very strong and very weak. An .85¢ U.S. Canadian dollar buys a lot more subscriptions and books than a .70¢ U.S. Canadian dollar. There was a time when this was a largely Canadian problem, but now librarians in the U.S. as well have had an unpleasant taste of what currency fluctuation and weakness can do to the purchasing power of library budgets. How much is enough? To go to our University administration each year with a dollar figure was becoming increasingly meaningless.

A *third* problem was that Western, like so many other academic libraries, had been forced to downsize, dropping positions and thus coping with a reduced staff complement. When the dollar was strong, my staff of 20 or so Collections Librarians was capable of generating purchase requests which far exceeded the processing capacity of a reduced Acquisitions staff. On the other hand, sudden weakness in the Canadian dollar would immediately translate into a sharply reduced trickle of orders going into Acquisitions, where staff would have so little work that they would be temporarily seconded to duties elsewhere in The University Library System.

So . . . what to do? Discussions with the University administration were fruitful, and we felt we really met with cooperation and understanding of our predicament. What we tried to do, then, was identify a more objective measure of "how much constitutes enough"–a corridor of adequacy, tied not to fluctuating currency rates but to a more objective sense of how much is needed to support teaching and research at Western.

In July of this year I left Western, or at least did so partially, to become Chief Librarian at King's College, a first-degree college affiliated with Western, having particular strengths in Religious Studies and Social Work, and supporting a number of interdisciplinary studies, plus a Master of Divinity program through its own affiliate College, St. Peter's. Obviously, the acquisitions budget is much smaller, but the same need seemed to exist to identify a corridor of adequacy. King's College students receive University of Western Ontario degrees, as do students in three other affiliated colleges, but King's Library is not part of The University Library System.

What I'm proposing here is principally a *methodology*, rather than any one way or even group of norms to be applied. What I have done is taken a number of measures and then examined whether, in the aggregate, they point to a corridor of adequacy in library acquisitions, which does seem to be the case, for a large university library system and for a small, baccalaureate college library.

ACQUISITIONS RATE AS A PROPORTION OF PUBLISHED UNIVERSE

Many of you will be familiar with the North American Collection's Inventory Project (NCIP), and its working tool the *RLG Conspectus*. For anyone who is unfamiliar, collecting activity is assessed at six levels–0 (out of scope) through 5 (comprehensive), which are tied to rough percentages of a possible universe of published literature in a discipline. These percentages are then further narrowed or broadened by the application of language codes (see Table 1).

In the case of Western, examination of written collections policies indicates that the great majority of departments and programs average out at a strong level 3, defined as being "adequate to support undergraduate and most graduate instruction,"[1] with some level 4 (research) collections in areas of particular strength and a few level 2 collections. Generally, level 3-4 collections predominate. With a few exceptions such as veterinary science and forestry, Western's programs cover a full spectrum of subjects in the arts, music, social sciences, science, medicine, technology and professional schools. Foreign-language material is a significant

TABLE 1

Level/Description of collection	% of published universe	Median percentage
5 (comprehensive)	80 - 100%	90%
4 (research)	60 - 80%	70%
3 (instructional)	40 - 60%	50%
2 (basic information)	20 - 40%	30%
1 (minimal)	0 - 20%	10%
0 (out of scope)	0%	0%

COLLECTING LEVELS PROPOSED
BY NCIP'S *RLG CONSPECTUS*

component of acquisitions in only a few programs such as visual arts, music, language and literature departments, etc. In 1991/92 production of new academic-level books in English in the US, UK and Canada was roughly 40,000 titles. Assuming that Western should be acquiring about 66.66% of that universe would suggest about 26,400 discrete orders per year. To that should be added another 3,500 or so foreign-language titles, for a total of roughly **30,000.**

In the case of King's College, a review of publication statistics provided by Blackwell North America and B. H. Blackwell (Oxford)[2] suggests a possible universe of publications of interest numbering some 7,300 titles. King's College's undergraduate offerings suggest an overall acquisitions rate of around 40% or 2,920 titles, to which should be added some 300 or so foreign-language titles, for a total of roughly **3,220** discrete orders annually.

POPULATION SERVED

"Every formula for library acquisitions ever created is essentially a political statement driven by voices within the library and user community," writes Charles Hamaker.[3] Many libraries use rough formulae of 10/5/1 or 8/4/2 or whatever variant of a/b/c, where a = number of discrete orders placed annually for every full-time faculty member, b = number of discrete orders placed for every full-time graduate student, and c = number of orders placed for every full-time undergraduate student (see Table 2). Such formulae are premised on the hypothesis that, while undergraduate circulations may be high, they are typically concentrated on a small percentage (circa 20%) of the collection, often on multiple copies. Faculty and graduate student use, however, is typically spread much less intensely over a broader and deeper spectrum of material, including more older, historical material, and a greater proportion of material in languages other than English. Typically, the formula is confirmed by or even based upon circulation statistics broken out by the three categories of users.

TABLE 2

Western

10	×	1,411	FTE faculty	=	14,110
5	×	2,012	FTE graduate students	=	10,060
1	×	15,994	FTE undergraduates	=	15,994
					40,164
					paid orders/yr.

King's

10	×	60	FTE faculty	=	600
1	×	1,725	FTE undergraduates	=	1,725
					2,325
					paid orders/yr.

POPULATION SERVED
USING A/B/C/ FORMULA

In the case of Western, an optimal 10/5/1 formula yields the following data:

10	×	1,411	FTE faculty[4]	=	14,110
5	×	2,012	FTE graduate students	=	10,060
1	×	15,994	FTE undergraduates	=	15,994
					40,164

A more conservative 6/3/1 formula produces:

6	×	1,411	FTE faculty	=	8,466
3	×	2,012	FTE graduate students	=	6,036
1	×	15,994	FTE undergraduates	=	15,994
					30,496

A worst case, minimal scenario[5] of one new discrete order per year, per user, undistinguished by category, would yield:

1 × 19,417 FTE users	=	19,417

What sort of data results from application of these formulae to King's? The optimal 10/5/1/approach suggests:

10	×	60	FTE faculty	=	600
1	×	1,725	FTE undergraduates	=	1,725
					2,325

HISTORICAL PRECEDENT

The following workflow data was provided by Western's Acquisitions Department:

Type of order	1989/90	1990/91	1991/92
Records output	48,643	39,251	29,433
Paid records output	41,566	**31,658**	23,721

From the point of view of The Library System's Collections Management Department, 1989/90 was a particularly good year, while 1991/92 proved to be a particularly tight one; 1990/91 was more of an acceptable median. An average of the three years suggests a minimally acceptable acquisitions rate of about **33,000** discrete paid orders annually.

At King's, annual acquisitions historical data is available for a much longer period of time:

Year	Books	Periodicals
1992/93	4,080	558
1991/92	2,536	536
1990/91	2,906	538
1989/90	1,839	546
1988/89	2,054	548
1987/88	2,278	550
1986/87	2,299	560
1985/86	2,822	588
1984/85	3,052	598
1983/84	3,110	583
1982/83	3,108	619
1981/82	3,249	555
1980/81	3,225	544
1979/80	3,002	507
1978/79	3,083	518
Average	**2,842**	**557**

CONVENTIONAL WISDOM

While it is certainly not "scientific," a certain "conventional wisdom" concerning a desirable acquisitions rate usually exists in most long-established libraries, such as those at Western and King's, and should not be ignored, as it is usually based on many years of insight and experience. Collections appraisals done over the years for various government agencies, new program initiatives, etc., have usually indicated good to excellent collections, suggesting adequate rates of acquisitions at both institutions, at least in the past. This conventional wisdom suggests that Western should be placing about 35,000 discrete orders annually for monographs and new serials, plus another 4-5,000 for non-book materials such as musical scores, sound recordings, realia and AV material for a total of roughly **40,000** discrete orders per year.

In the case of King's College Library, conventional wisdom has traditionally suggested an acquisitions rate of about **3,000** discrete orders for monographs and new serial volumes annually, with possibly a hundred or so more non-book items.

THE VOIGT FORMULA

The so-called "Voigt Formula"[6] develops an annual acquisitions rate premised upon programs offered at various levels and the nature of the literatures upon which they depend, ready geographic accessibility (or lack thereof) to other library collections locally or regionally, levels of funded research attracted by the institution, etc. Voigt also includes journals, which makes his formula more comprehensive than some. According to this approach, Western should be placing some **44,000** discrete orders per year. The model is intended for general universities with extensive advanced graduate (PhD) programs in a broad array of fields, with a number of professional schools, and posits a 40,000 volume base rate, to or from which multiples of thousands are added or subtracted respectively, depending upon the university's mix of programs, etc. Obviously, it is not applicable to small, liberal arts library collections such as those at King's College.

ARL COMPARISONS

Comparison with similar institutions has always been used as a norm of sorts, and undoubtedly retains some validity as a measure of adequacy. However, collections managers and library administrators should be aware of the "multiple mirror effect," which can result in inadequacies everywhere.[7] In other words, if everyone is poor, no one is poor, a sort of Soviet-style approach. Methodologies premised largely or entirely upon achieving economies do not necessarily address the need for continued growth and maintenance of physical quality and intellectual relevance essential to library collections, be they large or small. Account taken of the foregoing caveat, Western's University Library System supports a range of programs not atypical of any mid- to large-sized North American university, and comparison to the ARL median may therefore prove informative. The following data pertain to the hypothetical *median ARL institution*, and are taken from recently published statistics:

No. of current subscriptions:	15,614
No. of discrete orders placed:	**29,310**

CACUL STANDARDS

The Canadian Association of College and University Libraries (CACUL) has published a variety of standards over the years. One such report recommends a minimum collection of 100,000 volumes, beyond which the standard is based on the number of books per student (75 volumes per FTE student). Indeed, "the minimum figure of 75 volumes per student seems to have acquired iterative standing in Canadian academic libraries."[8] The same standard suggests norms for number of periodical subscriptions per student. ARL standards clearly do not apply to King's but various CACUL standards at least provide some guidelines

1,725	FTE	students	×	75	vols.	=	129,375
1,725	FTE	students	×	.75	periodical titles	=	1,293[9]

Application of the CACUL norm of 75 volumes per student and minimally acceptable acquisitions rate of 3% yields some **40,000** annual orders for Western:

2,012 FTE graduate students
15,994 FTE undergraduates

18,006	×	75 vols./student	=	1,350,450
1,350,450	×	3% annual growth	=	**40,513**

Application of the 75-volumes per student norm and the 3% annual acquisitions rate yields some **3,800** annual orders for King's:

1,725 FTE students	×	75 vols.	=	129,375
129,375	×	3% annual growth	=	**3,881**

A more recent standard, designed for Canadian College Learning Resource Centres, published as recently as 1992,[10] may have some relevance to King's College as well. The standard posits the following:

	Minimum Collection		Excellent Collection	
No. of FTE Students	Current Volumes	Serials Subscriptions	Current Volumes	Serials Subscriptions
1,000-2,999	60,000	600	90,000	1,200

and an annual growth rate of 3-5%. This standard would suggest that with its current collection of 90,376 books and 558 serial subscriptions, King's College has barely minimal collections in serials, but an excellent collection of books. An annual growth rate in monographs of 3-5% suggests an acceptable range of 2,711 to 4,518 titles, or an average of **3,614** titles using this norm.

CLAPP-JORDAN FORMULA

The well-known Clapp-Jordan formula deals almost exclusively with existing collection size, and does not really address the question of acquisitions rate, that is, in NCIP or Conspectus terminology, "current collecting intensity."[11] However, in the study of Ohio institutions from which their formula derives, Clapp and Jordan did consider the amount of the annual book fund, and recommended an acquisitions rate of 6%, thus following the lead of other writers of their time in their expectation of exponential growth.[12] Their acquisitions rate of 6% was based upon findings of Fremont Rider that, historically, research libraries doubled in size every sixteen years. In fact, they quote Rider's statement that

[t]his may be asserted as almost axiomatic: unless a college or university is willing to be stagnant, unless it is willing *not* to maintain its place in the steady flow of educational development, it *has* to double in size every sixteen years, or thereabouts.[13]

The result of this line of thinking was for many years the belief that libraries should have ever increasing acquisitions rates: the theory of exponential growth. Various percentages were adopted in long-range planning, ranging usually from 4 to 6%. It is obvious, now in the 1990s, that expectations of exponential growth are no longer realistic. Factors such as increased costs, decreased or steady-state funding, better bibliographic access, questions of access versus ownership, document delivery, and aggressive weeding necessitated by space limitations, and the physical deterioration of much acidic paper produced roughly between 1850 and 1950, together with the fact that the universe of scholarly publishing is no longer accelerating rapidly, have meant that very few large research libraries can seriously envisage exponential growth in the 1990s. It may nonetheless be informative to look at recent acquisitions rates at both King's and Western in this context.

Western					
Category	April 1990	Gross Adds	Net Adds	April 1991	% Growth
Volumes	1,634,481	57,173	41,447	1,675,928	2.54%

This 2.54% growth rate, well below the 4-6% range of formulaic approaches developed along Clapp-Jordan lines, would suggest current discrete orders of some **42,568** annually.

King's					
Category	April 1990	Gross Adds	Net Adds	April 1991	% Growth
Volumes	94,459	4,644	3,444	97,903	3.65%

At King's, continuance of a 3.65% growth rate would suggest current discrete orders of some **3,573** annually.

Nevertheless, we agree with Marvin McInnis, who found that existing, historical collection size, *in and of itself*, should not be a major factor in determining acquisition rate, for the reasons already mentioned which inhibit any expectations of exponential growth patterns in the 1990s.[14]

ACRL STANDARD FOR COLLEGE LIBRARIES

In 1986, the ACRL Board of Directors approved a set of standards prepared for it by the College Library Standards Committee. The standards include eight categories: objectives, collections, organization of materials, staffing, public service, physical plant, administration, and budget. The section on collections wisely notes:

> Once a collection has attained the size called for by [a] formula, its usefulness will soon diminish if new materials are not acquired at an annual gross growth rate of from two to five percent. Libraries with collections which are significantly below the size recommended in Formula A should maintain the 5% growth rate until they can claim a grade of A. Those that meet or exceed the criteria for a grade of A may find it unrealistic or unnecessary to sustain a 5% growth rate.[15]

Application of the norms for ACRL's "Formula A" suggests that Western has a grade A library system, and that therefore something well below 5% is reasonable as an annual growth rate (see Table 3). Western in fact experienced a 2.5% net growth rate of 49,737 volumes (41,447 titles), 1991 over 1990. This figure included gifts, theses, bound periodicals, etc. If one assumes that about 75% of these "net adds" were from discrete, paid orders, the figure would be around 31,085 titles. A 2.5% growth rate for Formula A as applied to Western would be **38,892** volumes per year.

In the case of King's, application of "Formula A" suggests holdings of 119,325 volume equivalents. In fact, King's holds some 106,877 volume equivalents, making it a grade A library in ACRL terms (it has 90% of recommended holdings). Section C of the ACRL standards states that "the extent of resource sharing through formal cooperative arrangements among libraries should be recognized in any assessment of the ability of a library to supply its users with needed materials."[16] As an affiliate college of The University of Western Ontario, King's can, in fact, offer its faculty and students

TABLE 3

Terms of ACRL (1986) Formula A	Western	King's
1. Basic collection	85,000 vols.	85,000 vols.
2. 100 vols. per FTE faculty member	141,100 vols.	6,000 vols.
3. 15 vols. per FTE student	270,090 vols.	25,875 vols.
4. 35 vols. per undergraduate major or minor field	17,500 vols.	2,450 vols.
5. 6,000 vols. per master's field, when no higher degree is offered	78,000 vols.	N/A
6. 3,000 vols. per master's field, when higher degree is offered	102,000 vols.	N/A
7. 6,000 vols. per 6th year specialist or professional degree field	12,000 vols.	N/A
8. 25,000 vols. per doctoral field	850,000 vols.	N/A
Total volumes:	1,555,690	119,325
3% annual acquisitions rate:	**46,670** orders/yr.	**3,579** orders/yr.
2.5% annual acquisitions rate:	**38,892** orders/yr.	**2,983** orders/yr.

ACRL STANDARD FOR COLLEGE LIBRARIES: 1986

full borrowing privileges at Canada's fifth-largest university library system two blocks away. King's own affiliate, St. Peter's Seminary, has a library with some 60,000 volumes, chiefly in the area of philosophy and religious studies, to which King's College patrons also have full access. Full document delivery service on a basis of 24-hour turnaround time is available among the four college libraries affiliated with Western. The library privileges attendant upon affiliation further confirm that King's is a grade A library. A 2.5% growth rate for Formula A as applied to King's would suggest **2,983** titles annually.

RATIOS OF MONOGRAPHS TO SERIALS

Unfortunately, most published standards refer to volume or title acquisitions rates, apparently largely monographic. Yet increasingly libraries are finding that ever larger portions of their budgets are tied up in ongoing commitments, largely serial in nature. Western's Acquisitions Budget Allocation Committee drew up ratios of serials to monographic expenditures by discipline for each of its seven libraries (see Table 4). These ratios are intended to prevent an entire acquisitions budget from being absorbed by escalating serials costs. The ratios were devised by discussions with faculty and by compar-

TABLE 4

Library	Serials %	Monographs %
Business	75%	25%
Education	55%	45%
Engineering	85%	15%
Law	90%*	10%
Music	45%	55%
Science/Medicine	85%	15%
Social Sciences/Arts	60%	40%

MAXIMUM SERIALS/MONOGRAPH
RATIOS BY LIBRARY PROPOSED
FOR WESTERN

*The high serials proportion allowable to Law is because so much of the collection is maintained by ongoing commitments to loose-leaf update services.

A library must not exceed its annual serials ceiling. If it does, cancellations are mandated the following year to redress the imbalance.

ing numbers of titles and dollar values for monographic and serial universes in each discipline. The universe for monographs was identified from statistics supplied by major vendors such as John Coutts Library Services, Blackwell North America, etc., and the representative serials universe from similar subject breakdowns of the Faxon Canada serials database. Once again, the principle of identifying a desired proportion of a published serials universe according to strength and importance of the programs given at Western *preceded* any translation of that universe into dollar values.

At King's College Library an "ad hoc" arrangement of charging serials subscriptions to monographic subject budget lines has, unfortunately, become institutionalized over the years on a significant scale. As library staff grapple with trying to determine what proportion of the acquisitions *really* goes into ongoing commitments, a similar look at approximate, desirable ratios of serials to monographs in different disciplines may prove informative (see Table 5).

A few examples may be helpful. Predictably, ratios indicated by the databases used suggest lower serials ratios in the humanities than in the social sciences or sciences. In each case, both monographic and serial, the subject was measured as a percentage of the total universe of publication used. Inevitably, the percentages would vary, depending upon the instrument used to identify the universe. For example, had the *Bowker Annual* statistics been used to measure the monographic universe instead of BNA's statistics; or *Ulrich's Plus* on CD-ROM, to measure the serials universe instead of the data provided by Faxon Canada from its universe. Nevertheless, we feel the indications–and that is all the ratios are–would at least be similar.

Using the example of *Psychology*, which represented 4.69% of the dollar value of the Faxon Canada serials database, but only 2.56% of the BNA monographs identified for its approval and announcement program, a ratio of serials to monographic expenditures of roughly **65/35** would seem appropriate. On the other hand, *Philosophy* represented 1.42% of the serials universe, but 3.57% of the monographs universe, suggesting a serials to monographic expenditure ratio of roughly 28/72%, rounded to **30/70%**.

Once ratios of this sort are determined for all or most subject

TABLE 5

Department	Serials %	Monographs %
English	15%	85%
French	20%	80%
Philosophy & Religious Studies	30%	70%
Economics	60%	40%
History & Political Science	33%	66%
Psychology	65%	35%
Sociology & Social Work	50%	50%

MAXIMUM SERIALS/MONOGRAPH
RATIOS BY DEPARTMENT PROPOSED
FOR KING'S

areas served by a library, it is possible to project an overall optimal ratio of expenditure, typically in the 40/60, 50/50, 60/40 range for an arts and social sciences library, with higher serials ratios in science, medicine and technology, and lower rates in libraries such as Western's Music Library, supporting a discipline purely in the humanities.

CONCLUSION

Rigid application of any of the foregoing approaches could well yield results which would be subject to question. However, in the aggregate, use of a half-dozen or more different approaches may point rather clearly to a desirable range of current collecting intensity for both monographs and serials (see Table 6). There is, moreover, a remarkable degree of consistency, despite the fact that the

TABLE 6

Approach	Orders/yr. Western	Orders/yr. King's
1. RLG Conspectus (proportion of a published universe)	30,000	3,220
2. Population served (10/5/1 formula)	40,164	2,325
3. Historical precedent at both institutions	33,000	2,842
4. Conventional wisdom	40,000	3,000
5. The Voigt formula	44,000	N/A
6. ARL comparison (median university)	29,310	N/A
7. CACUL standards	40,513	3,881
8. Clapp-Jordan formula	42,568	3,573
9. ACRL Standard for College Libraries: 1986	38,892	2,983
Average	37,605	3,117

RESULTS OF 9 DIFFERENT
APPROACHES APPLIED
TO WESTERN AND KING'S

points of departure are often quite different. The corridor approach suggests roughly **35,000** new paid orders annually for Western, and about **3,000** for King's. Collecting activity below the corridor of adequacy, especially if protracted over a number of years, would undoubtedly do irreparable damage to library collections, with direct implications for the credibility, even accreditation, of the programs they support. Purchasing power above the corridor of adequacy translates into problems: too much of a good thing, with serious implications for workflow and the creation of cataloguing backlogs (see Table 7). By merging corridors of adequacy for monographs and for serials, and tying these to average dollar costs,

TABLE 7

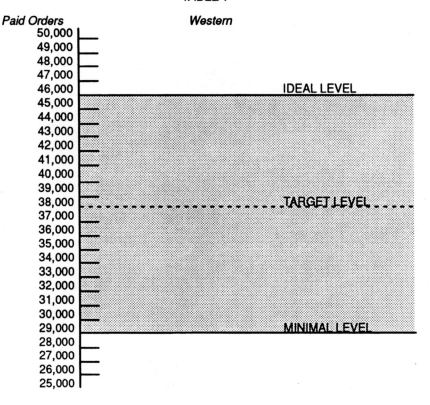

ACQUISITIONS: CORRIDORS OF ADEQUACY
FOR WESTERN AND KING'S

one can at least tie budgetary proposals to some sort of measurable, if flexible, universe beyond the apparently insatiable maw of the acquisitions budget itself. Administrators like the apparent objectivity of the corridor approach for, at least theoretically, it does suggest that at some point the library could–oh happy day–actually have ENOUGH!
Thank you!

NOTES

1. *NCIP Manual*, rev. ed. (Washington, D.C.: ARL/OMS, 1988), p. 19.

2. *Approval Program Coverage and Cost Study, 1992/93* (Lake Oswego, OR: Blackwell North America, 1993).

3. "Some measures of cost effectiveness in library collections," a paper presented at the Conference Library Acquisitions . . . (Oklahoma City, February 1991), p. 13.

4. from *Western Facts 1993* (London, Ont.: U.W.O., 1993).

5. Hamaker, p. 14.

6. Melvin Voigt, "Acquisition rates in university libraries," *College and Research Libraries*, 36 (1975), 263-271.

7. Voigt, p. 265.

8. CACUL. *Trends for the Seventies: Guidelines for Canadian University Libraries* (Montreal & Toronto, 1971), p. 40.

9. CACUL. University Library Standards Committee. *Guide to Canadian University Library Standards, 1961-1964* (1967), p. 19-20.

10. CACUL. *Standards for Canadian College Learning Resource Centres* (Ottawa, 1992), p. 13.

11. Verner W. Clapp and Robert T. Jordan, "Quantitative criteria for adequacy of academic library collections," *College and Research Libraries*, 26 (1965), 371-380.

12. *The Libraries of the State-Assisted Institutions of Higher Education in Ohio: Their Maintenance and Development, Guidelines for Policy* (Washington, DC: Council on Library Resources, 1964).

13. *The Scholar and the Future of the Research Library: A Problem and Its Solutions* (NY: Hadham Press, 1944), p. 9.

14. "The formula approach to library size: An empirical study of its efficacy in evaluating research libraries," *College and Research Libraries*, 33 (1972), 190-198.

15. "Standards for college libraries, 1986," *College and Research Library News* , 47 (March, 1986), 189-200. Virgil Massman and Kelly Patterson, "A minimum budget for current acquisitions," *College and Research Libraries*, 31 (1970), 83-88, consider the ACRL standards "[. . .] at best a questionable guide [. . .]," p. 83. More recently, see also David B. Walch's "The 1986 college library standards: Application and utilization," *College and Research Libraries*, 54 (May, 1993), 217-226.

16. "Standards for college libraries, 1986," p. 193.

Electronic Data Interchange (EDI): The Exchange of Ordering, Claiming, and Invoice Information from a Library Perspective

Glen Kelly

SUMMARY. Portions of this paper were presented as part of a panel discussion on the benefits of Electronic Data Interchange between libraries and book and periodical vendors. Other panelists in the discussion group represented the book and periodical supplier perspectives. The experience of Laurentian University's Library which has been using a proprietary format since 1987 to send electronic purchase orders to The Bookhouse in Jonesville, Michigan, and the current work they are doing with John Coutts Library Services Ltd., S&B Books, Bookhouse, Blackwells, Faxon Canada, Canebsco, and others in implementing the ANSI X12 BISAC approved 850 Purchase Order and the SISAC approved 810 Invoice transaction formats for serials invoices are featured in this paper.

INTRODUCTION

In 1987 Laurentian University Library began testing an electronic output file format to send purchase orders electronically to

Glen Kelly is Associate Librarian, Technical Services, at J. N. Desmarais Library, Laurentian University, Sudbury, Ontario, Canada P3E 1N9.

[Haworth co-indexing entry note]: "Electronic Data Interchange (EDI): The Exchange of Ordering, Claiming, and Invoice Information from a Library Perspective." Kelly, Glen. Co-published simultaneously in *Collection Management* (The Haworth Press, Inc.) Vol. 19, Nos. 3/4, 1995, pp. 77-94; and: *Practical Issues in Collection Development and Collection Access: The 1993 Charleston Conference* (ed: Katina Strauch et al.) The Haworth Press, Inc., 1995, pp. 77-94. Multiple copies of this article/chapter may be purchased from The Haworth Document Delivery Center [1-800-3-HAWORTH; 9:00 a.m. - 5:00 p.m. (EST)].

© 1995 by The Haworth Press, Inc. All rights reserved.

The Bookhouse,[2] a bookseller located in Jonesville, Michigan. Laurentian is located 550 miles north of Jonesville in Sudbury, Ontario Canada. After evaluation of the print image and fixed BISAC formats that were being used at that time we decided to develop a proprietary transmission format to ascertain if we could achieve more significant savings over the other transmission methods that were being used.

Based on the testing conducted we concluded that the cost of implementing the proprietary format that had been developed could be justified based on the savings we could achieve over the existing formats in use. The major reason for not choosing the fixed BISAC format was the additional cost of writing a translation or mapping program. The fixed BISAC format was more complex and lengthy than the simple database record structure employed in the proprietary format and because BISAC was fixed more information had to be sent with each record increasing the transmission costs.

The proprietary format was implemented and electronic ordering began and has continued successfully for both trading partners to this day. We are planning to test X12 transmissions with Bookhouse in the near future at which point we will stop using the proprietary format. In order to send orders a special output report format was developed based on the proprietary format that I developed and was incorporated as a special report in the Acquisitions module of multi-LIS software. Once orders were entered the report would generate only those orders for the Bookhouse and the electronic file created was forwarded to Laurentian's VAX EMAIL facility and a special EMAIL account was provided for the Bookhouse to pickup orders. Account privileges were provided to their own electronic mail account not to the library's database.

At first INET/2000 gateways were used to pickup orders as they were more cost effective than direct long distance connections. By 1990 direct long distance rates were less expensive and with the installation of 9600 baud modems the costs of transmission were dramatically reduced. In a previous article[3] published in 1990, electronic transmission costs for Laurentian were found to be significantly lower than the postage costs.

The comparison was based solely on transmission costs and did not factor in the savings in delivery time or the staff savings in not having to re-key the data at Bookhouse. Laurentian's primary gain was an average seven day improvement in delivery by using electronic ordering and Bookhouse was able to save time in processing Laurentian orders by not having to re-key the data which could then be forwarded directly to the publishers. Translation and mapping programs were written by Bookhouse to allow the electronic information to be loaded directly into their ordering software.

LITERATURE ON ELECTRONIC DATA INTERCHANGE

I have chosen a representative cross-section of literature on Electronic Data Interchange, teleordering, BISAC and SISAC standards for the most part pertaining to library interests, and have included the selective bibliography as an Appendix to this paper after the Notes section. I would like to refer readers to the Book Industry Systems Advisory Committee's *Implementation Guidelines for Electronic Data Interchange: EDI based on ANSI X12 Version 3.2.* A new manual is prepared each year as versions are approved for use in the Book Industry. The manual is a good starting point for the novice and expert alike and features all aspects from developing an implementation plan to the actual transaction sets that have been approved by BISAC.

THE MOVEMENT IN THE BOOK AND PERIODICAL INDUSTRIES TOWARDS INTERNATIONAL STANDARDS FOR EDI

The Book Industry Systems Advisory Committee (BISAC), the Serials Industry Systems Advisory Committee (SISAC) and their Canadian equivalents CBISAC and CSISAC have been working closely to develop and promote the use of ANSI X12 EDI transmission formats among booksellers, periodical agents, publishers, retail bookstores, and libraries. In Europe a similar process is underway with the EDIFACT transmission format (Electronic Data Interchange for Administration, Commerce and Transport sponsored by the United Nations Economic Commission for Europe). Current plans for the complete convergence of the two standards are scheduled for 1997.

Many booksellers, periodical agents, libraries, and Integrated Library Software Vendors aware of the scheduled convergence of the two standards have asked the question: why not wait until the two standards are the same and then implement EDI? What both trading partners, the library and the vendor, have to be aware of is that the standards are not written in stone. They continually change and are refined based on the needs of the industry they represent. Once X12 and EDIFACT are the same I will predict with absolute certainty, that the newly converged standard incorporating X12 and EDIFACT will itself continue to undergo changes. With this process of constant change and refinements in the standards will this not dictate constant programming changes to the trading partner's database software? The answer to this question is that the majority of changes to the standards can be resolved without any major programming effort by the trading partners, if they purchase third party X12 and EDIFACT translation and mapping software and do not attempt to hard code the X12 or EDIFACT into their own database programs.

THIRD PARTY X12 AND EDIFACT TRANSLATION AND MAPPING SOFTWARE

Mapping and translation software creating an X12 or EDIFACT format in the various versions that have been released is currently available from a variety of software vendors and will run on an MS-DOS based personal computer or on mainframes. EDI ASSET,[4] EDI/EDGE,[5] and X-Caliber EDI,[6] are examples of MS-DOS based software that are currently being used in the Book and Serials Industries. DEC/EDI and FileBridge[7] is a mapping and translation software package available for Digital Equipment. There are many more mapping and translation software packages that are available commercially. Most have training and hot-line support programs for an additional fee. Each package has a variety of features, some are easier to use, some are more expensive, some include PC communication software packages and some require that you purchase additional PC or mainframe communication packages. EDI ASSET requires that you purchase MIRROR III[8] communications software. It is important to mention that no matter what package is selected to suit your needs the X12 translation and mapping software package chosen will process outgoing and incoming X12 or EDIFACT transmissions using the specific version of X12 or EDIFACT that you have chosen to use with your trading partner(s). It is possible with some packages to have a variety of X12 versions maintained, one for each trading partner in cases where a trading partner may not wish to change to a newer version of X12 or EDIFACT immediately. Another helpful software product EDI EYE[9] allows the user to view all the versions of X12 industry wide.

IS IMPLEMENTING X12 OR EDIFACT SIMPLY A MATTER OF PURCHASING X12 OR EDIFACT TRANSLATION AND MAPPING SOFTWARE?

The purchase of appropriate X12 or EDIFACT translation and mapping software as well as appropriate communications software for a library PC or mainframe is only one of the decisions that has to be made. Creating the "flat ASCII" file from a library database requires that a special output report mechanism be written in most cases by the library's software vendor. Libraries with locally maintained database systems would be required to write their own output format. The output file is then sent electronically to the personal computer or the mainframe having the X12 or EDIFACT translation software where it is processed, and then forwarded to the supplier's database via modem either point to point, or by means of a Valued Added Network or VAN.

This part of the process is usually not that difficult or expensive for either a library software vendor or a library to write as most of the information is already available in the output program that is used to produce a printed purchase order. A more difficult and expensive programming effort, however, arises for both the library and the book or periodical supplier when they receive an X12 or EDIFACT transaction.

The X12 translation software will interpret the message and the information is easily located in a standardized format; however, then the real programming work begins to map the incoming messages into the library's or supplier's database software. This is a more lengthy and expensive programming effort. Once the mapping is finished for all the X12 or EDIFACT transaction sets (850 Purchase order, 855 Purchase Order Acknowledgement, 810 Invoices, etc.) there should be no need to change the input and output programs. Changes to the X12 and EDIFACT standards will be accommodated by the third party X12 translation and mapping software. Additional programming may also be necessary to accommodate trading partner decisions and relationships.

TRADING PARTNER DECISIONS AND RELATIONSHIPS

Trading partners decide what fields of information they wish to exchange in a trading partner agreement. There is no need to send all the Z39.50 MARC data to a trading partner unless that is part of the trading partner agreement. Information contained in MARC tags 005 Transaction Date, 020 ISBN, 069 Local control/Customer Order Number, 100 Author/Main Entry, 245 Title, 260 Publication Data/Imprint, 850 Quantity Shipped, 863 Enumeration and chronology (serials holdings), and 949 Customized Local Data would be sufficient for most purchase order transactions between trading partners. In many cases both the library and the trading partner already have the full bibliographic record for the item to be ordered in their own database directly from LC or other sources. X12 and EDIFACT are transmission standards or envelopes for communications and although they both have mandatory fields, and header and trailer information, trading partners have a great deal of freedom to decide what fields of information and how much information each field contains.

Generic forms can be used between trading partners, but specific forms can also be used in cases where less or more information has to be transmitted between partners. One library, for example, may require that multiple ship-to-addresses be used, whereas another library may only have one ship-to-address. Figure 1 compares an example of a Generic and a Specific form that could be used between trading partners. The field numbers used are for illustrative

FIGURE 1. Example of a Generic and a Specific Form that could be used between Trading Partners.

GENERIC FORM	SPECIFIC FORM
FIELD 1:	FIELD 1:
FIELD 2:	FIELD 3:
FIELD 3:	FIELD 4:
FIELD 4:	FIELD 6:
FIELD 5:	FIELD 8:
FIELD 6:	FIELD 9:

purposes only, and do not correspond to an actual X12 or EDIFACT transaction set.

AN EDI MODEL USING EITHER X12 OR EDIFACT FORMATS

The two-way flow of information between a library and a book or periodical supplier is illustrated in Figure 2. The first step is to create the flat ASCII file to be sent or received by the library or supplier's database. The second step shown is the use of mapping and translation software developed in-house, or by third-party vendors specializing in mapping and translation software, to create the X12 or EDIFACT communications formats. The third step is to send or receive the information using the X12 or EDIFACT communications format, directly via point to point modems or by using a VAN, to either the library or the supplier.

VANs provide both trading partners access to send and receive messages using electronic mailboxes. This feature allows a library or a supplier to dial-up the network only once to post and receive messages to a variety of suppliers or libraries, saving time for both parties. The TCP/IP protocol used by INTERNET is not X12 compliant, and currently requires manual intervention to address and receive the electronic envelope. Commercial value added networks allow X12 or EDIFACT transmissions to be sent to trading partners on the VAN with no manual intervention once the user has signed

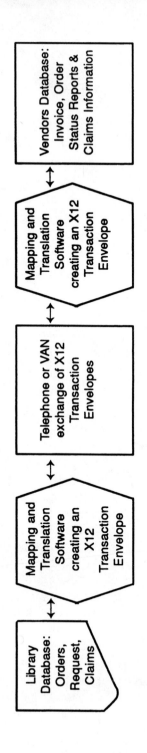

FIGURE 2. An EDI Model Using the X12 Communications Format

on to the network and the VAN also maintains an error log if the transmission is not successful. The X.400 international standard of VAN interconnectivity is supported by the major commercial networks like General Electric's Information Services (GEIS) and AT&T's Easylink networks. Messages on one VAN can be sent to another VAN reducing the cost of having to maintain accounts on more than one Value Added Network.

CURRENT TESTS OF X12 WITH BOOKSELLERS

In August 1993, Andy Marchewka, Senior Programmer assigned to this project by multiLIS and I were successful in sending our first trial order using the X12 850 Purchase Order Transaction set over the Canadian Telebook Network which uses the GEIS network to John Coutts Library Services Ltd. located in Niagara Falls, Ontario. Library staff have created a special test file of 100 orders so that I can measure the cost of sending orders over the network.

Unfortunately I must wait until I receive the bill containing the kilocharacter usage charge before I can provide you with the results. The basic monthly bill is under $8.00/month and the kilocharacter usage is billed at 30 cents per kilocharacter. This charge will vary on the number of transactions and records sent and received each month. DATAPAC charges to connect to the GEIS network are free of long distance connect charges; however, the highest speed of the public DATAPAC lines in Sudbury is only 2400 baud. Readers should be aware that transactions can be orders, order acknowledgements, claims, or invoices and that the real costs for such transmission will most likely be in the kilocharacter charges.

In the next month we intend to test the 850 Purchase Order Transaction format with a direct point to point connection with S&B Books in Mississauga Ontario and we will also attempt to send the same test file to John Coutts using INTERNET. The next BISAC transaction set we will test will be X12 855 Purchase Order Acknowledgement with John Coutts. We also plan on testing with all the major booksellers including Baker and Taylor, The Bookhouse, Blackwell North America, Midwest Library Systems and any other bookseller or vendor who is willing to do testing. As multiLIS has over 200 clients worldwide we are willing to test with as many suppliers as possible using both X12 and EDIFACT for our European clients.

CURRENT TESTING WITH SERIAL AGENTS

A project plan for the implementation of standard EDI among Faxon Canada, Laurentian University, and multiLIS has been signed. The project will start with Faxon Canada providing the latest version of the 810 Invoice transaction set containing Laurentian's yearly invoice to multiLIS so that the mapping process to the multiLIS payment module for serials can be started. Faxon Canada will be using EDI/EDGE translation software and we will be using EDI ASSET. Faxon Canada will be using the TRADEROUTE network and we will be using the Canadian Telebook Network or GEIS. We have been assured that there is VAN interconnectivity, but only live testing will confirm this statement. We have also agreed to begin testing with CANEBSCO, READMORE, and Blackwell England.

We expect that alpha testing will be underway this month and expect that the project will take one to three months to complete, including writing the program documentation, and integrating the EDI portion into the Acquisitions and Serials modules of the multiLIS software. Beta testing with other multiLIS sites will follow and we are planning to introduce some of the new EDI features next year.

CONCLUSION

The cost savings to both libraries and book and periodical suppliers using X12 and EDIFACT will more than compensate the one-time cost of programming associated with information mapping. The move towards EDI in other industries has already shown significant cost savings. Northern Telecom reduced their overall cost of processing a purchase order from over $50.00 to under $15.00 by implementing EDI.[10] What does it really cost your library to issue, claim, receive, and pay a bookseller or periodical supplier including the cost of your financial office that processes the cheques?

One important step before implementing EDI is to try to estimate the current costs, including staffing costs, to order, receive, and pay for library materials. You may be surprised at what it is currently costing to process a purchase order for payment. The real savings for libraries will be found in the staff time currently being spent to process claims and invoices and in the improved delivery times for purchases. The savings for booksellers and serial agents in not having to re-key information will more than offset the costs of implementing EDI.

The final stage of EDI is sometimes termed EFT or Electronic Funds Transfer. Moving business information between libraries and suppliers using standardized X12 or EDIFACT formats can be totally paperless, even the funds can be transferred without having to issue a paper cheque. Imagine not having to create a paper purchase order, mail or fax it to a supplier, receive a paper invoice and re-key the information into the library database, send the paper invoice for internal approval for payment, and then sending it on to your accounting office, who then re-keys the invoice data, which is then sent for another internal approval process, until finally a paper cheque is issued and is then mailed to the book or periodical supplier.

Implementation of EDI in industries like G.M., Ford, Chrysler, Northern Telecom, Provigo, Inco, and the Royal Bank to name only a few of the larger corporations has already made the entire process of purchasing, invoicing, and payment paperless with their trading partners. Libraries should be asking their library system vendors as well as their trading partners *when they will be ready to implement EDI using X12 or EDIFACT standards. Savings will only come to those trading partners implementing EDI!*

AUTHOR NOTE

The author is currently on sabbatical leave from Laurentian and is working in Montréal with the programming staff of multiLIS,[1] an Integrated Library System Software Vendor to implement the ANSI X12 and EDIFACT standards into the Acquisitions and Serials modules of their software. When the integration of the ANSI X12 and EDIFACT standards are completed multiLIS clients will have the ability to send and receive information electronically with their trading partners using the X12 BISAC and SISAC and EDIFACT standard transaction sets. Testing is currently underway with a variety of trading partners using point to point dial-up modems, Value Added Networks (VANs), and INTERNET.

NOTES

1. multiLIS™ is an integrated library software package available from Sobeco Ernst & Young Inc., 505 blvd. René-Lévesque West, Montréal, Québec H2Z1Y7.

2. The Bookhouse Inc. is a bookseller "serving libraries with any book in print" and is located at 208 West Chicago Street, Jonesville, MI 49250.

3. The comparative costs between the transmission formats tested can be found on pages 61 and 62 of my previous article entitled: "Exploring Costs of Electronically Transmitting Information Between a Library and a Vendor," *Information Technology and Libraries* 9:53-65 (March, 1990).

4. EDI ASSET is available from EDS (Electronic Data Systems Corporation) in both Canada and the U.S. and retails for over $3000.00 U.S. By special arrangement it is available to Canadian Libraries and members of the Canadian Telebook Agency for $299.00. The Canadian Telebook Agency's address is 301 Donlands Avenue, Toronto, Ontario, Canada M4J3R8, and EDS Canada Ltd. is located at 1615 Dundas Street East, Whitby, Ontario, Canada L1N7S6.

5. EDI/EDGE retails for $2500.00 U.S. and is available from DNS Associates, Inc., One Militia Drive, Lexington, MA 02173. This software package is also being resold by Faxon as a service to their customers.

6. X-Caliber EDI retails for $595.00 U.S. and is available from Patrick Frantz Consulting Ltd., 204 E. Jefferson Street, Syracuse, NY 13202.

7. DEC/EDI and FileBridge software is available from Digital Equipment Corporation, P.O. Box 4076, Woburn, MA 01888-9693. Total solution sets are available including training, start up services, and connection to a VAN that range in price from $26,000 to $45,000 U.S.

8. MIRROR III communications software retails for $139.00 in Canada and can be purchased at retail computer stores. Their address is Softklone Inc. 327 Office Plaza Drive, Suite 100, Tallahassee, FL 32301.

9. EDI EYE retails for $175.00 U.S. and is available from Sterling Software, 65 East 55th Street, New York, NY 10022. This software which is MS-DOS based allows the user to query and print all the X 12 versions of the transaction sets, and to query data elements and segments. This software package is extremely useful for programming staff to prevent coding duplication between transaction sets and versions and to understand the overall structure of ANSI X12 and the various industry subsets that are used with X12.

10. Kelly, Kathy. "The Potential of Electronic Data Interchange." Presentation given at the Ontario Library and Information Technology Association held May 27, 1993 in Toronto.

APPENDIX

ELECTRONIC DATA INTERCHANGE (EDI)
SELECTIVE BIBLIOGRAPHY

"Connecting with the booktrade: library use of TELEORDERING" *Vine* 73:19-23 (Dec, 1988).

"EDI or DIE" *Globe and Mail* (Issues for Canada's Future Supplement) (June, 1992), 20 p.

"Electronic Commerce: what's it all about?" *Globe and Mail* (Issues for Canada's Future Supplement) (March 11, 1993), 42 p.

"Focus on OSI: Electronic Data Interchange (EDI) Standards" *Universal Dataflow and Telecommunications Newsletter* 13:3-6 (Autumn, 1990).

"Teleordering" *British Book News* p. 90-91 (February, 1991).

"Wholesalers co-operate on electronic ordering" *The Bookseller* 4466:227-228 (July 26, 1991).

Barber, Joseph W. "Library-to-vendor electronic order transmission today: report of a telephone survey conducted in December 1988 for the Acquisitions Librarians/Vendors of Library Materials Discussion Group" *Library Acquisitions: Practice and Theory* 13 no. 3:275-279, 1989.

Barron, R. S. "Electronic Data Interchange & its Impact on Purchasing" Paper delivered to P.M.A.C. Sudbury (March 6, 1989) 11 p.

Bielenberg, W. Larry. "BISAC transmission at Concordia Seminary" Information Technology and Libraries 2:173-176 (June, 1983).

Blankenship, Edith. "Third Annual BATAB Users' Conference, 1979: Summary Report" Library Acquisitions: Practice and Theory 4, no. 3-4:225-230, 1980.

Blauer, Katherine. "BISAC Implementation at OCLC" *Library Acquisitions: Practice and Theory* 11, no. 4:363-366, 1987.

Bonk, Sharon. "Integrating Library and Book Trade Automation" *Information Technology and Libraries* 2:18-25 (March, 1983).

Book Industry Systems Advisory Committee. "Reports and Working Papers" *Information Technology and Libraries* 2:191-210 (June, 1983).

Book Industry Systems Advisory Committee. *Implementation Guidelines for Electronic Data Interchange: EDI based on ANSI X12 Version 3.2* New York: Book Industry Study Group, Inc., 1993. This BISAC X12 Manual is available from the Book Industry Study Group, Inc. 160 Fifth Avenue, New York, NY 10010-7000. Telephone: (212)929-1393, cost $150.00. This manual provides a series of useful implementation guidelines, and a glossary of EDI terms. The manual also includes the BISAC to X12 matrix used by the Publishing and Bookselling Industry, industry conventions for using X12 transaction sets, and the X12 transactions sets that have been approved for use by BISAC, namely: 810–Invoice, 840–Request for Quotation (For Permission to Photocopy Copyrighted Materials), 843–Response to Request for Quotation, 850–Purchase Order, 855–Purchase Order Acknowledgment, 856–Ship Notice/Manifest, 997–Functional Acknowledgment.

Bottomley, Lucy. "Electronic Data Interchange: standardization in the book industry" *Feliciter* 37, no. 6:5 (June, 1991).

Braun-Elwert, Rudolph. "Elektronischer Datenaustausch zwischen Erwerburg und Buchhandel: Der Elnsatz von Telekommunikation im Buchhandel" English translation of title: "Electronic data exchange between library acquisitions departments and the book trade: the introduction of telecommunication in the book trade" *ABI-Technik* 11:199-206 (3, 1991).

Bullard, Scott R. "Standards for Automated Acquisitions Systems: BISAC and SISAC considerations" *Library Acquisitions Practice and Theory* 11, no. 4:357-358, 1987.

Cargill, Jennifer. "On-line Acquisitions: Use of a Vendor System" *Library Acquisitions: Practice and Theory* 4, no. 3-4:235-245, 1980.

Cations, W. T. "Acquisitions systems and the book trade" *LASIE* 16:6-12 (Nov/Dec, 1985).

Cations, W. T. "Libraries and the book trade: electronic dialogue or discord?" *LASIE* 17:118-120 (Mar/Apr, 1987).

Chan, Sally & Ballance, Graigg. "Establishing Reliability in an EDI Environment" Paper presented to the Canadian Serials Industry Systems Advisory Committee (CSISAC) March 25, 1993 in Toronto. 20p.

Clapper, Mary Ellen. "Standards for Serials" *Serials Review* 12:119-131 (Summer and Fall, 1986).

Clapper, Mary Ellen. "The SISAC test report: results recommendations, what's next" *Serials Review* 13:7-11 (Fall, 1987).

Clapper, Mary Ellen. "Bar-codes, serial publications, and the SISAC Test" *Serials Review* 12:35-42 (Spring, 1986).

Cochrane, Tom. "Online ordering: report of a trial by the Queensland Institute of Technology Library" *LASIE* 17:110-116 (Mar/Apr, 1987).

Dove, Richard. "Teleordering and EDI in the book trade" *NEWSIDIC* 99:8-15 (February, 1990).

Ellis, Richard. "Electronic Ordering at UTLAS: A Chronicle of Library/Book Vendor/Bibliographic Utility Cooperation" *Information Technology and Libraries* 1:343-345 (December, 1982).

Fraser, Anne. "Serials librarians/serials suppliers: bridging the communications gap in the technological environment" *Australian & New Zealand Journal of Serials Librarianship* 1:45-55 (1990).

Godfrey, M. A. and Fenton J. "Online Ordering in a College Library using the OCLC Acquisitions Sub System" *Vine* 48:14-16 (May, 1983).

Hepfer, Cindy. "Everything you always wanted to know about SISAC (Serials Industry Systems Advisory Committee)" *Serials Librarian* 19: 211-212 (3/4, 1991).

Hicks, Peter. "Barcodes: stamping out human errors" *Advanced Information Report* 3-6 (November, 1990).

Hinnebusch, Mark. "METAMARC: An Extension of the MARC Format," *Information Technology and Libraries* 8 no. 1:20-33 (March, 1989).

Holmes, Philip. "The book trade as supplier and user of records" Chapter 5 of *Downloading Bibliographic Records:Proceedings of a one-day seminar sponsored by the MARC Users' Group* (Aldershot: Gower, 1986): 39-50.

Holmes, Philip. "Upgrading downloading" The Bookseller 4130:543-545, 547, 549-550 (Feb. 16, 1985).

Johnston, Patricia. "Using the microcomputer and electronic mail for acquisitions: let the machines do the work" *Bibliotheca Medica Canadiana* 11:146-147 (3, 1990).

Kelly, Glen. "Exploring the costs of electronically transmitting information between a library and a vendor" *Information Technology and Libraries* 9:53-65 (March, 1990).

Kristen, Herbert. "Erste Erfahrungen mit "DataSwets" an der Universitaetsbibliothek Karlsruhe" English translation of title: "First experiences with DataSwets at Karlsruhe University library" *Bibliotheksdienst* 22:522-524 (6, 1988).

Litchfield, Charles A. "Coded holdings: a primer for new users" *Serials Review* 14:81-88 (Spring, 1988).

Long, James. "Electronic Order Transmission" *Journal of Library Automation* 14:295-297 (December, 1981).

McKay, Sharon Cline. "The SISAC Bar Code Symbol" *Serials Review* 17:47-51 (2, 1991).

McKay, Sharon Cline. "SISAC, SICI and ASC X12: new standards for serials" *Australian and New Zealand Journal of Serials Librarianship* 2:29-35 (4, 1991).

Meilach, Dona Z. "Ordering slides via modem" *Online* 11:123-131 (November, 1987).

Mickos, Elisabeth. "IANI–future gateway for interlending communication" *IATUL Quarterly* 4:27-32 (March, 1990).

Miller, Amy. "Vendor's View of Library Automation Standards" *Library Acquisitions: Practice and Theory* 11, no. 4:359-361, 1987.

Mutter, John. "Parlez-Vous X12? Do you speak EDI? *Publishers Weekly* (Nov. 9, 1990) p. 27-29.

Nisonger, Thomas E. "Cost Analysis of the Libris II Automated Acquisitions System at the University of Texas at Dallas Library" *Library Acquisitions: Practice and Theory* 11, no. 3: 229-238, 1987.

Paeaekkoenen, Soile. "Kaeyttaejaen kokemuksia Suomalaisen Kirjakaupan lehtitilausjaerjestelmaestae" English translation of title: "The user's experience of the Finnish Bookshop's periodical subscription system" *Signum* 19:129-130 (July, 1986).

Paul, Sandra. "Computer-to-Computer Communications in the Acquisitions Process" *Journal of Library Automation* 14: 299-303 (December, 1981).

Paul, Sandra. "The Future of Standards" *Library Acquisitions:Practice and Theory* 12, no. 1:235-238, 1988.

Paul, Sandra K. "Bar coding for books–a new approach to machine-readable coding in the book industry" *EPB* 4:9-11 (January, 1986).

Paul, Sandra K. "Bar coding for books and serials" *EPB* 4:1,12 (February, 1986).

Paul, Sandra K. "Serial article identifiers–SISAC, BIBLID, NISO, ISO, ANSI and ADONIS: a confusion of alphabet soup" *Serials Librarian* 15:93-98(3/4, 1988).

Paul, Sandra K. "Bar code scanning update: modifications to the Bookland EAN recommendations" *EPB* 4:7 (November, 1986).

Paul, Sandra K. "Computers, libraries, and the book trade" *EPB* 3:3-5,12 (November, 1985).

Postlethwaite, Bonnie. "Publication patterns, the USMARC holdings format, and the opportunity for sharing" *Information Technology and Libraries* 9:80-88 (March, 1990).

Rauhanen, Tuula. "Akateemisen kirjakaupan tilausjarjestelmaet Atlax ja Alex" English Translation of Title: "The Academic Bookshop's ordering systems Atlax and Alex" *Signum* 19:129-130 (July, 1986).

Rowe, Richard R. "Serials automation and SISAC" *Library Hi Tech News* 1(8&9):1, 13 (Oct.-Nov., 1984).

Sabosik, Patricia. "SISAC: Standardized Formats for Serials" *Information Technology and Libraries* 5:149-154 (June, 1986).

Santosuosso, Joe. "Electronic Data Interchange (EDI) for Libraries and Publishers" *Bulletin of the American Society for Information Science* 15:15-17 (October-November, 1992).

Schwartz, Frederick E. "The use of Electronic Data Interchange (EDI) in the North American Library/Publishing Community: Current and Future Developments" Paper delivered on January 20, 1993 at "Information ONline & On Disk 93" in Sydney, Australia. 20p.

Somers, Sally W. "Standards! Standards! Standards! Experiences with Standards at the University of Georgia Libraries" *Library Acquisitions: Practice and Theory* 11 no. 4:367-372, 1987.

Stewart, Charles. "Update on Ordering Standards" *Information Technology and Libraries* 1: 341-343 (December, 1982).

Werner, Andreas J. "Standardisierter Geschaeftsverkehr: das projekt 'Elektronischer Datenaustausch zwischen Buchhandel und Bibliotheken auf der Basis von OSI (Open Systems Interconnection)'" English translation of title: "Standardized business: the project 'Electronic exchange of data between the book trade and libraries on the basis of Open Systems Interconnection (OSI)'" *ABI-Technik* 11:191-197 (3, 1991).

Ziegman, Bruce. "WLN Online Order Transmission" *Information Technology and Libraries* 1:346-348 (December, 1982).

EDI:
The Modern Way
to Do Business Together

John Cox

SUMMARY. In this paper I would like to deal with three aspects of Electronic Data Interchange within our community:

1. What EDI will do for publishers, vendors and librarians;
2. What are the practical consequences of implementation for each of us;
3. What is the current status of EDI development internationally?

WHAT CAN EDI DO FOR US?

The first thing to recognize about EDI, or Electronic Data Interchange, is that it is not new. Its origins can be traced back to the 1960s; but the first successful application is generally regarded as being the LACES system for clearing cargo at London's Heathrow airport in the early 1970s. However, several subsequent developments have been crucial to the widespread adoption of EDI: computers of enormous power including PCs, the enhancement of tele-

John Cox is Managing Director of B. H. Blackwell Ltd., Beaver House, Hythe Bridge St., Oxford, England OX1 2ET.

[Haworth co-indexing entry note]: "EDI: The Modern Way to Do Business Together." Cox, John. Co-published simultaneously in *Collection Management* (The Haworth Press, Inc.) Vol. 19, Nos. 3/4, 1995, pp. 95-105; and: *Practical Issues in Collection Development and Collection Access: The 1993 Charleston Conference* (ed: Katina Strauch et al.) The Haworth Press, Inc., 1995, pp. 95-105. Multiple copies of this article/chapter may be purchased from The Haworth Document Delivery Center [1-800-3-HAWORTH; 9:00 a.m. - 5:00 p.m. (EST)].

© 1995 by The Haworth Press, Inc. All rights reserved.

communications and, particularly, the liberalization and introduction of competition into telecommunications both in the USA and in Europe, have converged to facilitate data transfer between computers.

In the day-to-day process of transacting business, we create documents. A survey in the UK in the mid-1980s found that commercial documents cost up to $20 to process; over two thirds of this cost was associated with people and paper. For example, a library decides to order a journal subscription and enters details into its computer system. This system generates a paper purchase order, which is then dispatched by post to the supplier. The supplier, who is in this case a subscription agent, receives the purchase order and keys the details into their computer system. This system in turn generates an invoice which is then mailed to the library, and no doubt details of the invoice are keyed into the library's accounting system. This is a circular process where most of the same information is repeatedly keyed into a computer system in order to generate more documents. Similar repetitive flows of data go on between subscription agents and publishers.

We are not alone in our community. Cross-industry studies show that 70% of data that is keyed into a computer comes from another computer. It already exists in machine-readable form. Furthermore, when data is re-keyed there is an error rate of up to 5 percent. That is our current world, the world without EDI.

The benefits of eliminating this duplication of effort are obvious. Our problem is, particularly in the publishing, vendor and library communities, that we are less than clearsighted in concentrating on what EDI really is. It is about the processing of business transactions; it is not about delivering articles electronically. It is the automated computer to computer exchange of structured business documents between an enterprise and its vendors, customers or other trading partners. It is not on-line access, because this is interactive and involves the intervention of people. And it is not e.mail, because e.mail messages are unstructured strings of text, the format of which cannot be anticipated by the receiver. EDI is characterized by the batch file transfer of data in a highly structured and standardized format that both the sender and receiver can anticipate. In our community it concerns such transactions as purchase orders, acknowledgements, invoices and price lists. Because of the peculiarities of serials publishing, it also involves the exchange of data related to claims.

Many of the benefits of implementing EDI are quite tangible:

1. The reduction of paperwork and savings in clerical effort. There are the savings associated with one-time data entry, reduced error levels and improved error detection. Data that is delivered electronically can be stored on-line, eliminating the need for a paper copy. In turn, this means that management reports can be produced faster because all the data necessary is readily available in the computer. And reduced paperwork means reduced postage and reduced clerical workload. This will lead to staff savings and to the deployment of staff on higher grade and more rewarding activities.
2. The second principal benefit is that of speed. The rapid exchange of information electronically enables the library, the vendor or the publisher to get an instant and up-to-date view of any situation. For instance, a serials publisher can notify a subscription agent who can notify the library of publication delays, eliminating unnecessary claims.
3. The establishment of uniformity in communications between us will remove the difficulty and expense of providing proprietary links between one particular system and another. This in turn improves the availability of EDI literate data-processing staff and will tend to reduce costs in the future.

Those are the direct benefits. They flow from the application of technology to the process of doing business. Beyond those tangible benefits it is now apparent that the driving force behind EDI is its ability, as a management tool, to provide significantly better levels of customer service.

WHAT ARE THE PRACTICAL CONSEQUENCES OF IMPLEMENTATION?

Crucially, EDI is about "better business practice." It forces us to re-examine our processes and our trading relationships. EDI depends on getting it right the first time. It requires greater collaboration between customers and suppliers, and the need for maintaining standards at industry, national and international levels. We need more openness and less secrecy. We need to review old methods of working with a view to rationalization and simplification. The major challenge for all of us is not a technical one. The EDI challenge is one of changing the culture within our organizations and building trading relationships and understandings between all of us. Fortunately, within the publishing/vending/library community there is a spirit of co-operation which has already led to experimental projects between vendors and publishers and between vendors and libraries.

Within each of our organizations we have to evaluate the current state of in-house software and hardware for their ease of linking or converting to EDI. In particular, we have to deal with the personalities who will be affected. EDI is often seen as a threat to certain staff, particularly those within clerical functions such as administration, bookkeeping and logistics. These are all management issues which will arise in different forms in each of our organizations. There are two important areas that need to be dealt with: legal implications of EDI, and requirements for financial, technical and security audits:

1. *Statute law and case law are basically oriented towards information on paper.* The use of EDI clearly creates problems:

    a. Authentication is the first. If two parties trade with each other, they need to know each other's identity and to ensure that all transactions between the same two parties are as they should be. With paper-based documents this is easy; a letter-heading and a handwritten signature will suffice. EDI is different. The parties have to rely on electronic alternatives such as passwords, personal identification numbers, and transaction numbers.

    b. National and international trade often requires a large number of documents to be exchanged as part of the process. These "documents" may be required by law. An electronic document may not satisfy the legal requirement.

c. In the paper-based commercial world, many documents have to be kept in storage from anything between one to thirty years. Alteration of such documents can normally be detected. However, electronic data can be altered without detection depending on the form in which it is stored.

d. Reliability of EDI networks has implications for the legality of an EDI based transaction. The recipient of a message needs to know that he has received the complete message, that the message is accurate and that no data has been lost or added to.

e. There is always a risk that something will go wrong. Who will be liable? Are they insured? Liability could extend beyond the contracting partners to include network service providers, telecommunications companies, etc.

f. EDI brings with it the potential for fraud and theft.

g. We need to understand how legal contracts are established in the paperless trading world. This depends on how admissible electronically generated and stored data may be in court. It raises questions of the availability of such data to prove a case.

Much is being done to resolve these problems. The development of standards for EDI transactions includes checks to be made at the start and end of transmitted messages. Modern communications protocol such as X25 automatically check the sequence and safe delivery of packets of data. Moreover, the use of EDI can actually help to reduce the risks which create legal disputes, including the speedy dissemination of data along the supply chain, the transfer of data directly into the customer's own computer system and the ability to adjust prices instantly on both buyer's and seller's computers. In September 1987, the International Chamber of Commerce adopted the Uniform Rules of Conduct for the Interchange of Trade Data by Teletransmission (UNCID). These rules cover topics such as the correctness and completeness of messages, the position of intermediaries, identification and authentication, acknowledgement of transfers, confirmation of content, and the protection and logging and storage of data.

Probably the best way of dealing with these problems is to have "EDI Interchange Agreements." These will set the ground rules for the use of EDI between publisher and vendor, or between vendor and library. They will include defined rules for message standards, action to be taken on messages which are corrupt, or lost or illegally read, timing, insurance, security and identification, and which country's law should be applied to problems arising from international transactions.

2. EDI creates problems for the auditor. An essential element of any audit process is an audit trail. Clearly, paperless systems will involve much tighter record-keeping and controls. Within an EDI environment, the financial audit should be augmented by a security audit, and a technical audit.

A security audit should consider issues both internal to the organization, and external where a Value Added Network is used. This will include physical security, message authentication, confidentiality of data within the network, security of mailboxes, disaster contingency plans, and standards for international communications.

The technical audit is, of course, not unique to EDI. It simply provides an assessment of whether hardware or software within the system conforms to a specific standard or specification.

THE CURRENT STATE OF EDI DEVELOPMENT

We still have some competing national standards. In the UK we have TRADACOMS for the retail trade. In the United States the American National Standards Institute (ANSI) X12 has been widely adopted throughout the Americas, but has failed to make significant inroads outside this continent. One exception is our own journal community, where we have adopted X12 as the protocol internationally for transactions between publishers and vendors.

But this picture is rapidly changing. The United Nations joint EDI group, with members drawn from the US and Europe, has produced the first international syntax rules under ISO 9735 entitled EDIFACT–Electronic Data Interchange for Administration, Commerce and Transport. Continental Europe has already adopted

EDIFACT. Both ANSI and the appropriate authorities in the United Kingdom have resolved to migrate their own standards to EDI-FACT in due course. Meanwhile, companies like Blackwell's will have to be able to deal with EDI based in X12, TRADACOMS and EDIFACT. This is less a problem than it might appear, as EDI standards are conceptually quite close, although to machines they are mutually unintelligible.

Unlike the human brain, a computer is incapable of comprehending randomly presented facts and hence requires an intensely structured format to any dialogue it enters. There are a number of bodies that are hard at work in developing transaction standards:

a. ICEDIS is developing a range of transaction sets between publishers and subscription agents: price catalogue, dispatch data, order and invoice, cancellations, and, most important, claims and claim responses. Dispatch data is already published and operational. The other standards will all be confirmed and published during 1994. These transaction sets are all written in X12, by agreement between agents and publishers, wherever they are based.

b. Within America, SISAC and BISAC have in test or production a variety of X12 messages: claims from libraries, claims from subscription agents, and claim responses from subscription agents and from publishers, invoices, purchase orders, remittance advances, cancellations, and functional acknowledgements.

c. In Europe, EDITEUR is, somewhat later than its North American cousins, proceeding to develop transaction sets in EDIFACT. In this exercise, ICEDIS and EDITEUR are working closely together to ensure uniformity of approach.

We need to continue with the work on standards. We need to ensure that each of the bodies involved in setting standards collaborates with its counterparts to ensure uniformity. And our activities need to involve the systems vendors as well. Proprietary interfaces have proliferated. We need to ensure that our future efforts are devoted to the use of internationally agreed and recognized standards so that we establish a uniform communication structure between us and cut down on the cost inherent in writing machine specific software. So we have to bring the systems vendors into this discussion and pressurize them to recognize the utility and importance of EDI to their customers.

There is one other issue that is almost unique to the library community: the desire to use the Internet as the medium for EDI. With the advent of X400 PEDI standards, we need to investigate how the Internet can be used for EDI. Libraries do not want to pay for separate commercial services. If EDI is to be widely used, the problems of incompatible protocols (i.e., X12 and Internet's TCP (IP)) have to be overcome.

So where do we go from here? I want to go back to the beginning. EDI is not about technology, it is about the way we do business together. It requires the collaboration of different parties within our community, each of whom has different objectives from the other. We have to get our organizations to take on board the practical, legal and audit consequences of putting EDI into place. We have to involve our finance and computer services departments, not only internally, but in work with vendors and with publishers. Both vendors and publishers need to move beyond the establishment of standards to the practical implementation of EDI trading. And we have to get our systems vendors to get serious about EDI. If we can do all of that, we will make progress indeed.

APPENDIX 1

U.S. STANDARDS DEVELOPMENT ORGANIZATIONS

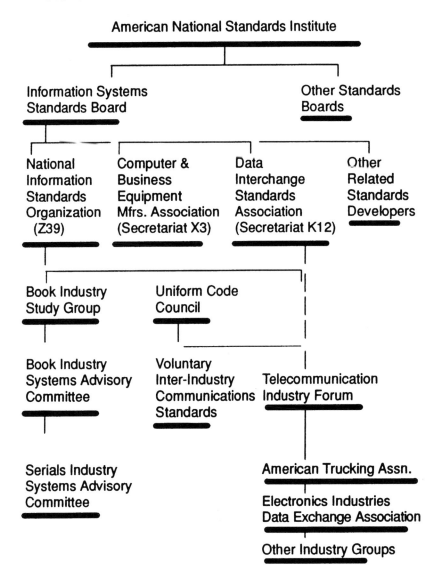

American National Standards Institute

Information Systems Standards Board

Other Standards Boards

National Information Standards Organization (Z39)

Computer & Business Equipment Mfrs. Association (Secretariat X3)

Data Interchange Standards Association (Secretariat K12)

Other Related Standards Developers

Book Industry Study Group

Uniform Code Council

Book Industry Systems Advisory Committee

Voluntary Inter-Industry Communications Standards

Telecommunication Industry Forum

Serials Industry Systems Advisory Committee

American Trucking Assn.

Electronics Industries Data Exchange Association

Other Industry Groups

APPENDIX 1 (continued)

U.S. STANDARDS DEVELOPMENT ORGANIZATIONS

This is an explanation of the acronyms shown in the organization chart

ANSI
ANSI coordinates all standards development within the United States. ANSI accredits standards development organizations and committees. ANSI represents the United States in international standardization through the International Organization for Standardization (ISO).

ISSB
ANSI assigns coordination for specific types of standards to its Standards Boards. ISSB has been assigned responsibility for standards in the area of Electronic Data Interchange (X12), Libraries, Information Science and Publishing (Z39), Computer Systems (X3) and related areas.

NISO, CBEMA, DISA
ANSI accredited the organization NISO to develop standards for Libraries, Information Science and Publishing. Accredited Standards Committee (ASC) X3 develops standards for Computer Systems using CBEMA as their Secretariat. ASC X12 develops standards for Electronic Data Interchange using DISA as their Secretariat.

BISG
BISG is the parent organization of BISAC and SISAC and is responsible for research of interest to the publishing community as a whole.

UCC
The UCC acts as the Secretariat for VICS. It is also responsible for the maintenance of the specifications for many bar code symbologies.

BISAC and SISAC
BISAC and SISAC develop book and serial industry-specific applications of the standards created by NISO and ASC X12. They also coordinate the application of bar codes for books and serials, all of which are maintained by the UCC.

VICS
VICS develops general retail applications of the standards created by ASC X12, as do the other organizations shown on the right of the chart.

APPENDIX 2

OTHER STANDARDS DEVELOPMENT ORGANIZATIONS and STANDARDS

BIG
Book Industry Communications in the U.K standardizes book-related transactions using the TRADACOMs format They are also involved in many areas related to standardization which are not specifically EDI.

EAN
The European Article Numbering Authority in Brussels is responsible for both bar code and EDI standards throughout Europe and the rest of the international community. Their EDIFACT subset is known as EANCOM.

EDIFACT
Electronic Data Interchange for Administration, Commerce and Transport. A syntax, sets of messages, data elements, segments, and codes for EDI developed by the United Nations Economic Commission for Europe (ECE) and subsequently approved by them and ISO.

EDITEUR
Electronic Data Interchange for Europe was formed two years ago. They are developing EDIFACT subsets for books and serials using the EANCOM subset of EDIFACT

ICEDIS
The International Committee on Electronic Data Interchange for Serials is a Committee of journal publishers and subscription agencies which have developed a unique, tape-based purchase order format and are working on X12 formats for other EDI transactions between these two types of organizations.

ISO
International Organization for Standardization is located in Geneva. ISO members are countries; ANSI represents the United States. Together with the International Electrotechnical Commission (IEC), ISO concentrates its efforts on harmonizing national standards all over the world. The results of these activities are published as one of the over 10,000 ISO standards. Among them are, for instance, the International Standard Book Number and Serial Numbers (ISBN and ISSN).

The Need for Library
and University Press Collaboration

Colin Day

INTRODUCTION

My given subject today is the Future of University Press Publishing. I could be predictive but instead I want to be prescriptive: suggesting ways in which we all need to be working together to bring about a future for the university presses that is in all our interests. A future that is not just desirable for the presses, but for all participants in the scholarly and academic process.

The central component of the route to my prescription is a recognition of close interdependence between libraries and scholarly publishers. In a sense we have all known that interdependence all our working lives: the publishers publish and for scholarly publication the libraries are the primary market. But usually this is the limit of our recognition of our interdependence; and in this society a commercial arms-length relationship has seemed proper, even preferable to any other closer relationship. By contrast I want to argue for a closer understanding and a joint working out of our mutual futures.

I am thus going to talk about change. And change inevitably brings with it the presumption that something is wrong with the way

---

Colin Day is Director of the University of Michigan Press, P.O. Box 1104, Ann Arbor, MI 48106.

[Haworth co-indexing entry note]: "The Need for Library and University Press Collaboration." Day, Colin. Co-published simultaneously in *Collection Management* (The Haworth Press, Inc.) Vol. 19, Nos. 3/4, 1995, pp. 107-117; and: *Practical Issues in Collection Development and Collection Access: The 1993 Charleston Conference* (ed: Katina Strauch et al.) The Haworth Press, Inc., 1995, pp. 107-117. Multiple copies of this article/chapter may be purchased from The Haworth Document Delivery Center [1-800-3-HAWORTH; 9:00 a.m. - 5:00 p.m. (EST)].

© 1995 by The Haworth Press, Inc. All rights reserved. *107*

we currently do things. Criticism rears its ugly head. I do not wish
to criticize either librarians or publishers but it may sound at times
as though I am. And because like most people I am more adept at
seeing the mote in your eye than the beam in my own, I fear that
some of you will hear what I am saying as a criticism of the library
community. This is NOT my intention.

Indeed, I strongly believe that we must consciously and energeti-
cally eschew criticism of each other and devote our energies to
exploring common interests and developing collaborations.

SYSTEMS THINKING

We must look at the system by which scholarly writing moves
from scholar-as-author to scholar-as-reader as a totality–as a system. In the recently published book *The Fifth Discipline*,[1] Peter
Senge argued that we must be sure, in seeking solutions to problems, that we look at the whole system and not just at one component.

I believe that Senge's way of looking at processes is very appo-
site for examining our mutual position. We need to look at the joint
endeavor of university presses and academic libraries as a system.
We must not pursue the apparent best solutions for each of us
separately without considering the total system in which we jointly
operate.

To show the nature of Senge's approach, let me first show a
simple but persuasive example that he has developed.

Figure 1 shows the separate decision processes of the two super
powers engaged in a nuclear arms race. We see each logically
proceeding from a perception of the situation to a conclusion about
appropriate action to ensure their individual security.

But now combine these two processes into a single diagram
(Figure 2) and we see how the two interact and feed on one another
to subvert the increased security that the two players each expect
logically to follow from their individual actions.

This is an example of how essential it is for us to look at the
whole system.

Just to show a simple application of this approach to our mutual
predicament, let us look at the price spiral effect.

FIGURE 1

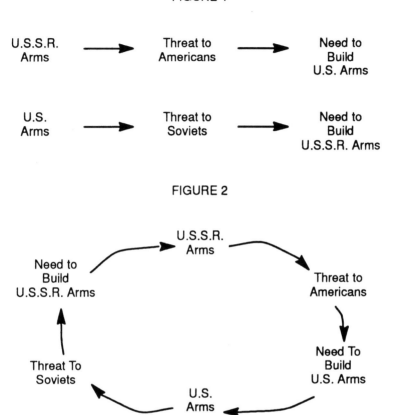

FIGURE 2

Figure 3 shows the separate reactions of the two players–libraries and presses–each pursuing their own concerns. Now again let us link them into a system. Figure 4 shows again how a view of the whole system reveals that the two players are undermining each other's actions and producing a perverse and unhelpful result.

When we look at the system as a whole, we see that, to quote Senge, "in many systems, 'doing the obvious thing does not produce the obvious desired outcome'." Indeed each participant does the obvious and rational thing but the system-wide result is unforeseen and perverse.

In fact, of course, we are embedded in a much more complex

FIGURE 3

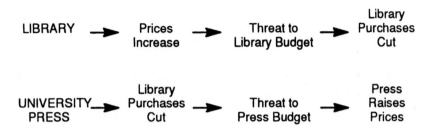

FIGURE 4

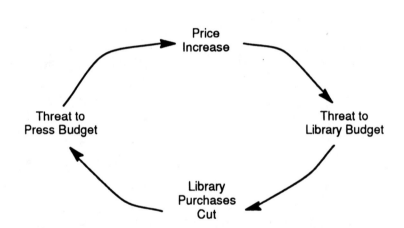

system than that, a system which involves both faculty and university administrators. My purpose, though, is not to present some complex model of the whole system. I just want to persuade you that we all have to take a broader view, a system-wide view.

LINKS IN THE SYSTEM

What I now want to do is to look a little more closely at two of the mechanisms that drive the simple circular system I have sketched out in Figure 4. I want to show that those mechanisms are powerful and, importantly, are becoming more powerful. We are on a circular route to perdition.

The Importance of Library Purchases

The first point in deconstructing the working of the system is to persuade you of your importance.

You are not just important customers for academic publications. You are, for much of that range of literature, the dominant customers. A group that is surely buying 50% and probably much more of the copies of most specialist academic titles has great influence.

This would not be so significant if libraries were behaving in very different ways so that the actions of one library were countered by the different actions of another. But all university libraries are experiencing the same kinds of pressures and dealing with those pressures in similar ways. Indeed similar actions are not only occurring coincidentally but in an organized way as university administrators urge libraries to get together and coordinate their collection policies. We are now seeing action not just in parallel but in concert.

So I want to persuade you that libraries, as they coordinate their actions, are having actual and substantial impacts on what gets published and at what price. Each librarian may feel that he or she is making separate and rather small decisions, purchase by purchase, but the cumulative effect is substantial and serious.

Simply, if you buy less of a journal or a category of book, the publisher's expectations for future sales decrease. They have basically three responses to this: they can raise their prices to compensate, they can cut their costs (and a likely implication of this will be some reduction in quality), or they can get out of that business.

Now, I am not criticizing the thinking that lies behind libraries' decisions to cut purchases. This is the natural and rational response to the situation that you face. But somehow we have to take the total system, not our particular perspective, into account. We need to work together to point out to university administrators and faculty that budget stringencies have implications that are serious for scholarship. And that they have to think about these problems in a broader context in which the availability of publishing outlets for faculty writings and the supply of academic publications are all interlinked with issues of library and university press financing.

Publishing Costs

I suspect some of you are thinking that you have heard all this from publishers before. Despite what the publishers say the publications keep coming anyway. But, as I have remarked already, the extent of resource sharing that is now being planned is of a quite different order of magnitude from that which we have lived through so far. To explain why I believe the present situation is different and more acute than in the past, I have to delve a little more deeply into publishing costs and explain one central fact about the economics of book and journal publishing.

The fact is: it takes a large amount of money to get ready to make the first copy of a book or journal and a very small amount of money to make one more copy. This was nicely recognized in the Mellon Report *University Libraries and Scholarly Communication*.[2]

What does this say? As the publisher can expect to sell fewer copies of a book, so the same first copy costs must be shared over fewer copies. The burden on each copy therefore increases and the price sufficient to cover those costs must increase. This is what we have all been experiencing for a good number of years.

I want to show one picture (Figure 5). It is a diagram of the average cost of making a book as the quantity manufactured changes. In fact this curve does not include all the first copy costs but it shows the effect starkly enough. Not only does the cost per copy rise as the likely sales figure decreases, but the rate at which that cost rises, increases as the expected sales level decreases. At the right hand end of the graph, the fall in sales from 1000 to 900 produces a modest increase in the average cost—the kind of increase that we can perhaps absorb by increases in efficiency. But from 600 to 500—let alone 300 to 200—the increase in cost is much larger, far beyond what we can hope to absorb by efficiency gains. And for many more specialized works, we are now looking at sales as low as that.

The presses have not just accepted this situation. As first copy costs have loomed larger in our calculations, we have striven to get

FIGURE 5

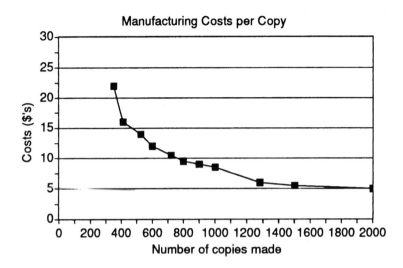

them down: in the last ten years, we have about halved the staff time to produce a new title; we have been far ahead of commercial publishers in using authors' discs to economize on typesetting; we are now pioneers in editing on screen to further reduce those first copy costs. But all these efforts and innovations are not sufficient to counter the effect of shrinking sales. And the effect is becoming more acute.

Unable to use efficiency gains to cope, what else can a university press do? We could argue for a greater subsidy from our university. We can cut some dimensions of quality—doing less editing, for example. But increasingly presses are addressing this problem by reducing their publishing in the fields where sales have dropped to these very low levels.

The simple arithmetic of declining sales is getting us rapidly towards a point, if we are not there already, where cost increases outstrip any means we have for compensating. We are facing a new situation that demands your attention and concern for the present state of scholarly publishing.

So far I have been in the black ink on white paper mode talking of a traditional technology. But note what is distinctive about electronic publishing over the net: nearly all the costs are now first copy costs and it would seem that the marginal cost of one extra copy is now zero or close thereto. In other words, the problems that follow from high first copy costs and low replication costs are if anything magnified in the electronic environment. Now it is not my purpose today to go into the subject of electronic publishing in any detail. But I did want to make that point and discourage anyone from thinking that issues about which I am talking will disappear once we get to electronic publishing–they will not.

One likely response to the argument so far would be to suggest that there is plenty of fat in the publishing system to cope with these kinds of cost increases. This is not so. It is true of hardly any organization publishing thoughtfully and with discrimination in the humanities and social sciences. The university presses for example do not aim to make profits but price on a cost recovery basis. Many of the publishers with whom you deal as academic librarians are living on the financial brink.

So far I have presented an argument as follows: because of budgetary stringency libraries have been forced to economize on their purchase of materials. This has meant a significant decrease in total sales of the average academic book. In many fields we are now at a point where the cost consequences of those recent decreases and certainly of any future ones are beyond the ability at least of the university presses to absorb. This is different from the past decade or two where productivity gains on the one hand and tolerable price increases on the other have permitted us to keep publishing despite the continual slide in the market.

Again let me briefly digress onto electronic publishing. Although I think there are more problems in publishing long linear documents electronically than the visionaries suggest, accepting that we will go that route for many academic books, will this be the panacea? We see something like a 20 to 30% reduction in our costs by the elimination of the physical artifact. It is only of that magnitude because as I said earlier most of our costs are first copy costs and few of those are dependent upon the final medium in which the text is embedded. So there is no panacea in electronic publishing, and there are many problems, especially economic ones, yet to be solved.

FAIR USE

So far I have formed my arguments in terms of reductions in purchases by libraries. One of the means by which libraries strive despite the financial pressures put upon them to give a good service to the communities is by vigorous use of the doctrine of fair use. My thinking in this area was greatly helped by an article by Nina Matheson. One sentence particularly caught my eye. She wrote:

> We fought . . . for the Fair Use provisions . . . that would maximize the interlibrary sharing of resources and assure students and teachers ready access to the information that they need.[3]

On first reading that seemed perfectly reasonable. But then it dawned on me that it is a *static* remark. No one can argue with it with respect to materials already in the libraries. The more those already published materials can be shared the more people can benefit from them.

But what of the *dynamic* aspect? By this I mean the flow of *new* materials that scholars and teachers will need in the *future* and that *future* scholars and teachers will need, materials that have not yet been published. Might maximum fair use endanger the availability of new material for the libraries and for the scholars and students whom they serve?

I believe that maximum employment of fair use can have that effect and that library policies must take this dynamic aspect into account if they are to "assure students and teachers ready access to the information they (will) need" tomorrow. Libraries can no longer take for granted the supply of materials for them to collect or not collect as they choose. Their selection decisions feed back into the publishing process and close off publishing avenues for certain types of book and journal.

Recognition of this poses difficult problems. Libraries are cutting purchases and sharing resources for obvious and rational reasons. As budgets get tighter, as more of those budgets are eaten up by STM journals, as the need to buy hardware for electronic publications and pay high lease or subscription charges for various kinds of data resource, something has to give. Monographs are not purchased and journal subscriptions are canceled. Document delivery services and interlibrary loan become more and more crucial to your operations. No one can criticize the libraries for these actions which are forced upon you by financial stringency.

While the libraries are acting thus, the university presses seeing shrinking sales are cutting their academic publishing. Their response to the situation is also rational and also difficult to avoid. And so I come back again to the need for a system-wide approach to our problems.

CONCLUSION

It is hard not to wonder if things are organized sensibly when two entities owned by the same institution–the university–are each pursuing policies that make life more difficult for the other. Might not our parent institutions try to reconsider this at the university level rather than the independent unit level? And find some more reasonable way through the problems with which we are each faced?

While we were merely jointly stoking a price spiral, the impact was limited. But now sales of monographs are reaching levels where publication is becoming exceedingly hard to sustain for whole fields of the humanities. The impact therefore is now beginning to reach the faculty who can no longer find publishers for their books, nor have easy access to the works of their colleagues. The flow of knowledge is beginning to falter. And universities face interesting problems of tenure and promotion when the expectation that the young scholar will have published one or two books is setting an increasingly unattainable standard.

Do I exaggerate the present? Yes, to some degree. The number of publications in major fields has probably not yet fallen and there is undoubtedly an argument for some small reduction in the number of academic works published. But in minor fields publishers are definitely pulling back, and even in a field as large as English literature, there are many worthy works that are finding it hard to find a publisher. And that problem will increase.

The basic message that I have been trying to put across is this. We cannot any longer take the flow of academic publications for granted. Libraries, as the dominant purchasers of academic books and journals, are not just cutting what they choose to purchase, they are also cutting what is available for them to purchase. Resource sharing can mean resource disappearance. Does this matter? I believe it does. We are university press publishers and academic librarians because we believe that what scholars do is central to the values and sustenance of our culture. We want to play our part in the continual development and dissemination of the work of scholars–of human knowledge. We share the basic values. But by viewing our problems separately, we are endangering that greater activity and we must find joint solutions that recognize each other's constraints and concerns but seize the possibilities that being parts of the one institution–the university–offer for combined and therefore better solutions.

NOTES

1. Peter M. Senge, *The Fifth Discipline*, Doubleday, 1990.
2. Anthony M. Cummings et al., *University Libraries and Scholarly Communication: A Study prepared for the Andrew W. Mellon Foundation*, 1992, p. 95.
3. Editorial, *Bulletin of the Medical Libraries Association*, 81(3), July, 1993.

Copyright:
An Internship

Eleanor I. Cook

The reason I am here today is to talk about an internship I completed as part of a masters degree in leadership and higher education at Appalachian State University. The genesis of the idea was formed at this conference two years ago when the then CEO of the Copyright Clearance Center, Eamon Fennessy, was in attendance. Mr. Fennessy's comments during an audience discussion sparked me to ponder on the idea that perhaps the CCC was an organization that librarians ought to know more about. At the time, I knew that I would be required to do an internship for the masters degree I was working on, so I thought, "wouldn't that be an interesting place to go!" So, I took the opportunity, between sessions of the conference, to talk with Mr. Fennessy about the idea.

Mr. Fennessy's reaction to the proposal was quite welcoming and encouraging. A few weeks later I received a letter from him, urging me to pursue the idea. I saw this as a positive beginning. It was a full year and a half before I actually began the internship. In the meantime. Mr. Fennessy left the CCC and Isabella Hinds, Manager of Professional Relations, became my major contact for the remainder of the experience.

To set up the internship, a certain amount of intense preliminary

Eleanor I. Cook is Serials Librarian, Appalachian State University, Belk Library, Boone, NC 28608.

[Haworth co-indexing entry note]: "Copyright: An Internship." Cook, Eleanor I. Co-published simultaneously in Collection Management (The Haworth Press, Inc.) Vol. 19, Nos. 3/4, 1995, pp. 119-124; and: Practical Issues in Collection Development and Collection Access: The 1993 Charleston Conference (ed: Katina Strauch et al.) The Haworth Press, Inc., 1995, pp. 119-124. Multiple copies of this article/chapter may be purchased from The Haworth Document Delivery Center [1-800-3-HAWORTH; 9:00 a.m. - 5:00 p.m. (EST)].

© 1995 by The Haworth Press, Inc. All rights reserved.

contact was required. This was challenging because I had a full plate of responsibilities to deal with as serials librarian at ASU. Meanwhile, the folks at CCC were focused on their mission. Consequently, there were moments of doubt and frustration. A lot of work went into establishing what amounted to a tenuous relationship. During the entire process, I was never confident that the internship would get off the ground. In fact, I did not receive final feedback from Ms. Hinds until the week of this conference. Fortunately, everything worked out and I have been generally pleased with the results.

Next, I'm going to tell you a bit about the internship experience itself–I won't belabor it, but I know some people are interested in this aspect. Then I will cover what the Copyright Clearance Center is in general, and what it means to libraries.

There have been a number of librarians interested in doing internships with other players in the information chain. Some of these individuals have been active in an American Library Association/ALCTS initiative to establish a formal program with publishers and material vendors. The Copyright Clearance Center is unique because it does not fit into any of the traditional categories. In many ways, CCC is a vendor, but not like those with which we in the acquisitions field are familiar. They *do* provide a service, however, and my internship provided an opportunity to learn more about an organization that is gaining prominence in our community.

In terms of doing an internship related to a degree program, let me share a couple of observations. I was treated as a graduate student, not as a professional librarian who was holding a full-time job and also going to school. An internship arranged through a professional organization such as ALA or NASIG might have provided me with better introductory credentials. Because of having to go it on my own, I do not think I got the same consideration and support I might have otherwise. That is a minor criticism. I was doing this internship for academic credit, so I had to press on sometimes even when I was frustrated. I had to complete the requirements to receive a grade. If I had been participating in the internship simply as an intellectual exercise, the pressures would have been less intense.

I work for a non-profit institution of higher education and

although the Copyright Clearance Center is also a non-profit organization, their corporate culture is more like that of a profit-oriented business. For instance, I was asked to sign a non-disclosure agreement, which basically restricts me from commenting on how much money CCC collects and who pays whom for what. I signed the agreement without hesitation because I assumed I would not have access to that sort of documentation. As it turned out, I did actually see financial statements that were confidential via annual reports and other internal communications left behind in the office space I occupied. The figures I saw were not any big surprise, however, and the details were not my concern.

A positive aspect of the internship was the question of how I was going to live while I was staying thousands of miles from home. I had visions of camping out in a hotel room; this was something I wasn't looking forward to having to do. Fortunately, a woman who works for CCC in the corporate licensing division offered me a guest room in her home. This arrangement worked well for several reasons: one, she worked in an area of the company with which I would have little contact; and two, she was a rich source of information about the company's social culture, and also about the region in general. As a hostess, she was extremely generous and flexible with her time and space and the stay was quite pleasant because of her hospitality. I felt that my hostess assisted me in seeing the organization in a more human context. I seriously recommend that if you ever consider doing an internship, that you try to make such an arrangement.

Let me tell you about the primary mission of the Copyright Clearance Center. After the 1976 revision to the U.S. copyright law, the CCC was set up as an independent organization to assist with the collection of copyright royalty fees. Over the years, CCC's primary mission has been to centralize the process as much as possible. While not every publisher in the U.S. is registered with the Copyright Clearance Center, the CCC constantly works to sign up more publishers as they can. Except for a certain amount retained to cover overhead, CCC passes back the rest to publishers and other copyright holders.

The Copyright Clearance Center is not responsible for determining who should pay. I believe this is a major area of misunderstanding. The CCC is not the "copyright police." They are simply a pass-through agent. Publishers and their legal counsel have the real concerns about compliance. That is not to suggest that the CCC isn't involved in educational efforts regarding copyright. However, CCC does not generally address the issue of fair use. It is their contention that activity that falls into "fair use" does not fall into their purview.

The Copyright Clearance Center's procedure for handling permissions is extremely complex. They wish to make the system easy for people to use, but it is far from simple.

If the CCC's primary mission is to collect copyright fees, then their secondary mission is to collect and charge fees in a timely manner. Users of copyrighted material need quick turnaround and there is still work to be done on this aspect. The delays one might find aren't because the researchers (several of whom are librarians, I might add) aren't responding fast enough but because they are working with a moving target. The database that CCC has built includes information on a multidimensional scale. As a serials cataloger in a research library, I was used to dealing with title changes, but CCC researchers also must keep up with publishers who constantly change their permission fees, plus those who sell rights and partial rights to other publishers!

The Copyright Clearance Center's user population is diverse. There are three programs to meet their needs. The corporate licensing program covers the largest client base. These customers are sampled and then assessed a yearly fee based on a complex formula. Larger companies often pay a hefty fee. The Texaco law suit centers around this sort of activity. The question remains: should for-profit companies be allowed to invoke fair use rights under certain circumstances? The Texaco case is still under appeal, and the end result could have great implications for other populations, such as the non-profit sector.

Another program offered by CCC is the Academic Permissions Program (APS). This program is geared toward processing permissions specifically related to coursepacks and classroom anthologies. CCC aims for a two-business-day turnaround for these requests. The Kinkos lawsuit settled this issue a few years ago.

A third system of permissions-gathering is called TRS–Transactional Reporting Service. This system covers other possibilities not covered by the first two mentioned. This is the avenue most often used by library interlibrary loan departments, individual document suppliers, and corporate document delivery vendors. There is a range of very large to very small, individual customers represented. With this service, the copyright fee is paid after the fact, in a "pay-as-you-go" fashion, using log sheets.

The Copyright Clearance Center has also ventured into developing an academic licensing system, but the progress of this has moved slowly, and still is in the pilot stage. CCC wanted to see if universities could benefit from such a system and used a handful of schools as test sites, but the results have been inconclusive. It simply may not be worth the effort. Much of the copying activity at a university falls under "fair use," so it may not be efficient to monitor such usage.

There is a new area that will have impact on the Copyright Clearance Center's viability. The management of electronic copy and scanning rights represents a whole new set of parameters. Therefore, I believe that it is very important for universities to develop comprehensive copyright policies as soon as they are able. This will lay the groundwork for future developments, especially in the electronic arena. While doing my internship, I designed a survey and talked to a random group of librarians, attorneys, and print shop managers, on various campuses. Although my sample was limited, I easily concluded that most institutions did not have an overall plan coordinated by one area of campus. Instead, what I discovered is that with a few exceptions, institutions of higher education have fragmented policies; that is, different areas within the same institution control different aspects of copyright regulation. They often do not communicate or understand their common interests.

University attorneys are usually the key administrators to gather data on this situation. Our university attorney at ASU, for instance, has been keenly supportive of such efforts and is drafting a revised institution-wide document with the help of this research and other input.

What else is in store for the future of CCC? For one, they are developing a CD-ROM version of their huge permissions manuals.

These tomes are big enough to earn a place next to the national union catalogs!

In conclusion, what are the contentious issues in this presentation? First, if CCC wishes to involve academic institutions more heavily in their programs, they need to have us represented in greater numbers on their board of directors. Second, CCC needs to grapple with the issue of fair use; they should acknowledge its legitimacy in certain circumstances, and join us in reaching a common understanding.

Finally, CCC needs to listen to outside consultants and others about their leadership and management skills. I see a definite lack in this area that needs to be addressed. There are some fine people working for CCC; however, there just may not be enough of them at the appropriate levels. Also, there is no one working at CCC with a good understanding of how a typical university operates.

I believe that the Copyright Clearance Center has a future if it transforms itself into a service-oriented organization. I get the impression that some librarians think that the CCC is a pawn to commercial publishers. That is definitely not the case; the CCC serves many other constituencies and trying to pay attention to all their concerns is a challenge. There are many opportunities for the CCC to continue to play a role in the information chain—it will be up to them to accept the challenge.

Reference Works in Science:
Revolutionary Evolution

William E. Russey

Scientists generally, and chemists in particular, are the beneficiaries of a remarkably comprehensive and well-organized literature base. This is, of course, no accident; to practice science implies extending the limits of existing knowledge, and this in turn presupposes the availability of a reliable and efficient means for determining that which is already known–more precisely, what has already been recorded. The fact that chemistry has been unusually successful in achieving access to its knowledge base is also no accident, but rather a consequence of the unusual precision with which a "chemical fact" can be characterized once it has been reported in the primary literature.

The most obvious way to summarize and further disseminate new information after it appears in the literature is through an abstracting medium. Indeed, several professional organizations have at various times undertaken the development of comprehensive abstracts of the chemical literature, but only one such product has survived: the American Chemical Society's *Chemical Abstracts*, now prepared with active cooperation from chemical societies worldwide. For many years, *Chemical Abstracts* and its associated indices commanded a prominent place in the personal libraries of

William E. Russey is Professor of Chemistry at Juniata College, and Editor of Ullmann's *Encyclopedia of Industrial Chemistry*.

[Haworth co-indexing entry note]: "Reference Works in Science: Revolutionary Evolution." Russey, William E. Co-published simultaneously in *Collection Management* (The Haworth Press, Inc.) Vol. 19, Nos. 3/4, 1995, pp. 125-130; and: *Practical Issues in Collection Development and Collection Access: The 1993 Charleston Conference* (ed: Katina Strauch et al.) The Haworth Press, Inc., 1995, pp. 125-130. Multiple copies of this article/chapter may be purchased from The Haworth Document Delivery Center [1-800-3-HAWORTH; 9:00 a.m. - 5:00 p.m. (EST)].

© 1995 by The Haworth Press, Inc. All rights reserved.
125

individual research chemists, especially academics, but by the 1950s the publication had grown to such an extent that an individual subscription had become an anachronism. More recently, the burden of maintaining a complete set of *Chemical Abstracts* shows signs of becoming intolerable even for large university libraries–despite the fact that chemists quite properly insist that instant access to all the abstracts is absolutely essential to their work.

By 1992 the world's chemical literature had flourished to such a degree that the *abstracts* of one year's worth of information were consuming six running-feet of shelf space! To complicate matters further, abstracts alone are worthless in the absence of a set of comprehensive indices, and while the first ten years of *Chemical Abstracts* (covering the period 1907-1916) could be indexed in four volumes with a total of 4800 pages, the *9th Collective Index*–covering the *five* year period 1972-1976–takes up 12 running-feet of library shelving. The cost of processing and distributing this information has of course increased correspondingly, one of the reasons why many libraries–and chemists–are increasingly being forced to consider alternative ways of accessing the primary literature. The library at Juniata College, where I teach, abandoned the printed versions of the *Chemical Abstracts* collective indices more than a decade ago, committing itself at the same time to establishing and maintaining a reliable computer link to the central *Chemical Abstracts* database in Columbus, Ohio.

Chemical Abstracts of course represents only one part of the equation. Other more specialized reference works attempt first to classify and then selectively evaluate this mass of chemical information in order to provide more rapid access to a reliable and comprehensive set of facts–facts that in most cases also appear in the abstracts, but without any qualifying commentary, and distributed almost randomly. The most important examples of this more organized form of comprehensive chemical information originated in Germany in the 19th and early 20th centuries. They include Beilstein's *Handbuch der organischen Chemie,* Gmelin's *Handbuch der anorganischen Chemie,* Landolt and Börnstein's *Zahlenwerte und Funktionen aus Physik, Chemie, Astronomie, Geophysik, und Technik,* and Ullmann's *Encyklopädie der technischen Chemie,* a work with which I have personally been affiliated for the past several years. These reference sources have also experienced the extreme pressures that accompany an exponential growth in the number of recorded facts. Each has been forced to respond in more or less creative ways to a rapidly changing set of circumstances, especially as libraries–and chemists–increasingly raise questions about the wisdom of maintaining multiple approaches to the same information, and of shelving thousands and thousands of printed pages that–in any particular library–will *never* be consulted, simply to ensure that certain crucial (but unpredictable) pages will be instantly available the moment they are needed.

Electronic data processing has long been perceived as one of the keys to resolving the literature dilemma. *Chemical Abstracts* began experimenting with electronic processing of information during the 1960s in an almost desperate attempt to cope with what had become a mountainous backlog of unprocessed articles, and *Chemical Abstracts* also played one of the pioneering roles in providing direct consumer access to a publisher's electronic data files. An early consequence was the development of "on-line" literature searching, an expedient that–properly conducted–virtually eliminates the need for tedious, inefficient, and ultimately unreliable manual review of multiple sets of printed indices. Depending on the nature of the search, the various "hits" that result might also be the subject of on-line examination, especially if they are few in number; alternatively, abstracts identified as relevant, or even the source documents themselves, can simply be ordered for conventional express delivery. The Beilstein Institute has similarly engaged in an active program of electronic data-retrieval development, creating systems uniquely applicable to its own database of information on organic compounds, in part as a way of ensuring the continued viability of this rare and fragile source of specialized knowledge.

Quite naturally, the editors and publishers of the Ullmann's *Encyclopedia of Industrial Chemistry* have given considerable thought to the potential inherent in electronic data management, although in this case the challenge is a rather different one. While the *Encyclopedia* does constitute a significant source of numerical and factual data, which obviously must remain current if it is to be useful, the principal task of Ullmann's is to provide authoritative narrative accounts of chemistry as it applies to an incredibly wide range of commercial materials and processes, at the same time reflecting the diverse expertise–and varied writing styles–of hundreds of specialists from throughout the world. Information of this type is meant to be browsed, read, and absorbed, and it is clearly not well adapted to the standard techniques of traditional on-line data access. At the same time, however, such an encyclopedia is poorly served by revisions released in the form of printed supplements. The current (fifth) edition of Ullmann's was initiated over a decade ago, but it will not be complete until 1996, by which time the early volumes will already be seriously out of date.

The traditional response to this problem would be to begin now to plan for a sixth edition, despite the fact that many fifth-edition entries might actually require relatively little change. Preparing a completely new set of the Ullmann's would represent a massive commitment: the fifth edition will comprise 36 volumes of about 700 pages each, and the editorial effort involved in its production is extremely demanding and time consuming. Furthermore, experience suggests that at least a few of the yet-to-be-recruited new authors are sure to prove inferior to their predecessors, and production costs are continuing to rise at an alarming rate.

For these reasons and others, VCH Verlagsgesellschaft and the Ullmann's editorial team have elected instead to take the first steps leading in a completely new direction: transforming the existing electronic data files constituting the fifth edition of the *Encyclopedia* into a perpetual "living *Ullmann's*" based on the latest CD-ROM technology. What we envision is a reference tool incorporating all the information and flexibility associated with the traditional hardcopy product, but enhanced in ways that are consistent only with an electronic substructure. One important benefit from the librarian's point of view is the fact that a work now occupying six feet of shelf space will in the future be contained within a single compact disk, which can in turn be accessed by several users working simultaneously at networked remote data-processing terminals. At regular intervals–probably annually–and at relatively modest cost, the entire work will be replaced on a subscription basis by a new disk offering a substantially revised data base: with more recent production figures, the latest insight into current and projected industrial practices and trends, and new versions of key articles deemed to be either weak or obsolete. Rather than constantly struggling to create entire new volumes, a highly trained editorial staff would suddenly find itself free to devote exclusive attention to the systematic review and perfection of an existing body of information.

The concept seems to us to be an exciting one, and it is almost certainly feasible, but if it is to succeed, an extraordinary amount of attention will need to be devoted to the precise nature of the electronic end product. In particular, a truly "user-friendly" interface will be essential. "User-friendliness" has long been of special concern to the Ullmann's staff, reflected in an unusual level of attention to editorial and stylistic consistency, extensive indexing and cross-referencing, and a concerted emphasis on lucid writing. The projected "electronic *Ullmann's*" must not be allowed to suffer in this respect–indeed, its convenience should actually be enhanced by the provision of new tools for maneuvering within the work (jumping instantly from a reference number to the corresponding literature citation, for example, or following the lead of a cross-reference to a different article altogether), and by the provision of new ways of locating information, including searches based on logical combinations of search terms, the use of "wild cards," and direct access from a variety of indices. We also foresee a need for straightforward means of storing intermediate search results electronically for possible subsequent review and printing; for a "zoom" capability to facilitate close on-screen scrutiny of illustrations and tables; and for several approaches to generating hard copies of selected passages or articles. The latter operation would normally be accomplished in-house, but the publisher might continue to play a useful role in the case of more extensive or exacting demands.

What I have been describing here is admittedly still a dream, but it is a dream in the process of being realized. Commitment and enthusiasm on the part of the publisher have been assured, and a prototype in the form of an "Ullmann's CD-ROM Index" has already been prepared and demonstrated last month (at the Frankfurt Book Fair). Such an index actually offers more advantages than might be immediately apparent: lower cost relative to the printed version, simultaneous multiple-user access, complex search regimens, and the possibility of obtaining from a local work station an annotated list of relevant entries to be examined later at one's own convenience in the library. A demonstration model of the full-fledged Ullmann's *CD-ROM Encyclopedia* is expected to be ready for preliminary evaluation at the next Editorial Advisory Board meeting in June, after which suggestions and critical comments will be actively solicited throughout the world from potential users–especially chemists and engineers, but also librarians representing various types of institutional settings.

All of us who are associated with this development–editors, production staff, software developers, and marketing personnel–are enthusiastic about the prospects, which we see as relevant to reference publications in virtually every discipline, and we warmly welcome whatever critical insights and observations you might choose to provide.

The European Publishing Community and the European Electronic Environment

Charles Germain

INTRODUCTION

Due to the large number of panelists I limited this presentation to two issues regarding the dynamics at work in the European publishing community. Other issues, as for example the emergence of University Presses, will be for another time. The two issues for this morning are: (1) the European process, and (2) the electronic environment.

THE EUROPEAN PROCESS IN THE FALL OF 1993

There is good news and bad news on the European front.

The bad news first:

Last year I was reporting here the initial problems with the European Exchange Rate Mechanism and the predicted fall of the British pound and the continued erosion of the other European currencies versus the U.S. dollar.

Katina asked me to update this paper.

Well, it's going to get worse for the European currencies.

Charles Germain is Chief Executive of Gauthier-Villars North America, Inc., 875-81 Massachusetts Avenue, Cambridge, MA 02139.

[Haworth co-indexing entry note]: "The European Publishing Community and the European Electronic Environment." Germain, Charles. Co-published simultaneously in *Collection Management* (The Haworth Press, Inc.) Vol. 19, Nos. 3/4, 1995, pp. 131-139; and: *Practical Issues in Collection Development and Collection Access: The 1993 Charleston Conference* (ed: Katina Strauch et al.) The Haworth Press, Inc., 1995, pp. 131-139. Multiple copies of this article/chapter may be purchased from The Haworth Document Delivery Center [1-800-3-HAWORTH; 9:00 a.m. - 5:00 p.m. (EST)].

© 1995 by The Haworth Press, Inc. All rights reserved.

131

After 15 years of providing some currency stability, the Exchange Rate Mechanism, in fact, has collapsed in August 1993.

Before August 1993 most of the European currencies (Belgian franc, Deutsche mark, Danish krone, French franc, Irish punt, Luxembourg franc and Dutch guilder) had to keep within narrow bands of 2 1/4 % around their central parity rate, whereas the Spanish peseta and Portuguese escudo had a leeway of 6%. The British pound and Italian lira had already left the ERM in the battles of September 1992.

Now only the Deutsche mark and the Dutch guilder are formally held to their old limits. Other currencies can move around their central parity rate up to 15%, which means that they can move away from each other up to 30%!!

Basically, from a European point of view, we are back to 30 years ago.

The consequence for U.S. libraries is that European publications are going to be cheaper. Furthermore, if the Clinton administration succeeds in reducing the national deficit, with the economy recovering, the Federal Bank will increase the interest rates. The U.S. dollar then might not only increase but recover the historical heights of 1984.

Many countries in Europe are going to be free to jump-start their economy with lower interest rates, which will ultimately decrease the value of their currency.

Even the stronger European currencies such as the Dutch guilder and the Deutsche mark, with Germany holding on to its high interest rate to suppress the inflation resulting from its huge deficit after reunification, even these currencies should decrease versus the U.S. dollar.

The bad news for European publishers, as for every European manufacturer of goods and services, is that the instability of currencies is going to be followed by the instability of the markets.

The currency dislocation can ultimately become a serious threat to completion of Europe's 3 trillion dollar single market.

The other bad news is that as a consequence the Maastricht Treaty is inapplicable, except in regard to Germany and The Netherlands.

In the other countries, the currencies are fluctuating too much to envision a single currency in the near future.

So what next for Europe?

Instead of "deepening" itself through Maastricht, Europe could widen with the admission of Eastern European countries as well as the four richer nations (Austria, Finland, Sweden and Norway) that are negotiating to join.

Anyway, the European idea has survived 10 years of Charles de Gaulle in the sixties and another 10 years of Margaret Thatcher in the eighties, so we can believe that it will continue to survive because the European fabric is still at work.

Everywhere the European fabric is still at work. That is the good news. The European idea is too large and potent to be measured in decades.

In our industry, publishers and librarians have remarked how much scientists all over Europe are regrouping and restructuring their national associations into large entities and how many societies and society journals are created every year with the term European in the title, such as the European Journal of Bla Bla Bla.

In July 1992 we had in Paris the first European Congress of Mathematics. The European Society of Mathematics already existed, but they never had a joint meeting.

These are the 1991 numbers of individual members by country of origin. As we can see, for the European Society of Mathematics, the European concept is much larger than the EEC:

22	British (Scottish)
13	Danish
359	French
8	Georgian
112	German
11	Irish
174	British (English)
9	Luxembourg
49	Norwegian
17	Polish
22	Portuguese
41	Swiss
29	Dutch

In 1992, 1300 mathematicians met in Paris, from 58 different countries. Five mathematicians were distinguished with the Fields Medal, the highest distinction in mathematics (there is no Nobel Prize).

Objectives of the Meeting

1. To communicate between mathematicians the most recent results of their research.
2. To foster dialogue between mathematics and the social fabric in Europe.
3. To stimulate cooperation between European mathematicians at the personal and institutional level.

- 300 mathematicians in 5 days presented their research in poster sessions.
- We had 39 workshops and 10 plenary conferences in the Grand Amphitheatre of La Sorbonne.
- 25 other meetings took place as pre-conferences and post-conference meetings.
- 16 panels gave mathematicians an opportunity to meet with other scientists and scholars.
- More than 200 sponsored trips, including room and board, were offered to scientists from Eastern Europe who could not afford the expenses.
- 2 exhibitions and a mathematical movie festival scored a large success with a larger audience.

The next meeting is planned for 1995.

What we see happening here is a copy of the American Mathematical Society in Europe.

In the frame of the European Process and the failure of communism, which by definition was controlling all exchange of ideas, there is in Europe, all over Europe, a huge need for scientists to meet, and therefore to create in Europe the type of organization such as the AMS, ACS, APS, ASPP, ASG, CS, etc., which will create a set of standards of quality and foster communication, exchange, and stimulation between large groups of scientists.

What was impossible at the country level is now possible at the

European level: to create large and strong cross-border non-profit societies of scientists, with more working capital and international vision, which will have the credibility to lobby the different national governments, to harmonize their education and research systems, invest in those areas, help the poorest institutions meet with the rich ones, and talk academia out of its traditional, narrow national context, as has been for too long present in certain fields of science in France and other countries.

THE ELECTRONIC ENVIRONMENT SEEN FROM A EUROPEAN PERSPECTIVE

As is the case in North America regarding primary research journals, the electronic technologies only have an impact for the distribution, not for the format of the journal itself.

There are currently in North America only 41 electronic primary journals: 38 of them are free, and most of them are not even peer-reviewed.

We see the same situation in Europe. On-line peer-reviewed primary journals are only in the experimental phase, whereas secondary publications and reference tools are flourishing on CD-ROM. The full impact of new media is on secondary publishers ("repackagers"), not on primary publishers.

In fact, primary publishers are not committed to the printed media. On the contrary, most of them do not own their printing facilities. They subcontract the printing process. The commitment of a primary publisher is to the information itself published, not the media.

And there is a very strong interest in electronic technology.

Interests

First, their interest is a response to the strong library interest and good-will towards new information technologies all over Europe.

Second, primary publishers understand that there is a shift from journals ownership to article access, at least for the part of the library collection called peripherals.

Third, we see the emergence of electronic networks in the scientific community and its development into global communication highways.

Fourth, scientists are more computer literate and very soon the so-called "nintendo generation" is going to be in our faculties and labs.

Fifth, I see what I call the Gold fever, or the "Gold Rush." You hear things like: "Something dramatic is going to happen, a guy with the right product at the right time is going to make it and become very rich, let's be among the first to follow him, with our wagon and tools." Every one would like to be the Robert Maxwell of the next century.

But in spite of this strong interest towards new media, we see at the same time underlying forces that are definitely slowing down the development of new products.

One, you hear: "Let us serve efficiently the community and make an honest living out of it, instead of looking good because you are losing big bucks on the cutting edge."

Two, publishers are worried about some librarians' misconceptions:

- misconception #1: Access to articles is going to be cheaper than ownership of journals.
- misconception #2: Electronic storage is much more cost effective than shelf space.
- misconception #3: Paper is expensive.
- misconception #4: Vendors and publishers are going to be the conservators.
- misconception #5: Research and development costs for entry into new media are easily manageable.

Three: The delivery of articles versus journals ownership equals for the primary publisher business cannibalism, not new business revenue. And so far, publishers have seen very little money coming from the CCC or the DD suppliers.

Four: The DD market is already very competitive, so competitive that it is scary. Publishers worry about the future of this industry.

Five: The notion of "fair use" of electronic products has still to be defined.

Six: The technology is not yet here 100%. New media gurus are also perceived as highly paid SOBs who don't understand the economics of primary publishing.

Seven: The economical models, as well as the legal and organizational models are to be set up.

Eight: Nobody has answers to the question of the critical mass of data that is going to clog the communications highways.

Nine: The mission of primary publishers is to be global, and not all of the continents are ready for new media.

So in a Few Words

The deepening of the European process has slowed down and will probably give place to a widening process. Also it appears that we are entering a new period during which the U.S. dollar is getting stronger versus the European currencies.

* The European process on the west front and the changes of the east front are forces at work to foster the development of large societies of scientists.
* It is clear that primary journals in their majority will be maintained in their printed forms in the years to come, even if they will be repackaged for distribution into electronic format, once the economic, legal and organizational models are in place.

APPENDIX 1

MAJOR FACTORS IN FAVOR OF ELECTRONIC PUBLISHING

* STRONG SUPPORT FROM LIBRARIANS

* SHIFT FROM JOURNALS OWNERSHIP TO ARTICLES ACCESS

* EMERGENCE OF ELECTRONIC NETWORKS AMONG SCIENTISTS

* SCIENTISTS ARE MORE AND MORE COMPUTER LITERATE

* GOLD RUSH EFFECT

APPENDIX 2

UNDERLYING FORCES SLOWING DOWN THE DEVELOPMENT OF NEW ELECTRONIC PRODUCTS

* FEAR OF FAILURE

* LIBRARIANS' MISCONCEPTIONS

* THE CURRENT ECONOMICS OF DD AND ILL DON'T WORK FOR PUBLISHERS

* THE DOCUMENT DELIVERY MARKET IS ALREADY VERY COMPETITIVE

* THE NOTION OF "FAIR USE" OF ELECTRONIC PRODUCTS IS ILL DEFINED

* THE TECHNOLOGY IS NOT YET HERE 100%

* NO ECONOMICAL NOR LEGAL NOR ORGANIZATIONAL MODELS

* CRITICAL MASS OF DATA ON THE NETWORK

* DISCREPANCIES BETWEEN CONTINENTS

APPENDIX 3

CORPORATE MEMBERS OF THE EMS

The list below gives the founding full members of the European Mathematical Society (EMS). In some cases, membership is conditional on ratification by the society's ruling body.

Austrian Mathematical Society
Belgium Mathematical Society
Bulgarian Mathematical Society
Union of Czech Mathematicians & Physicists
Union of Slovak Mathematicians & Physicists
Danish Mathematical Society
London Mathematical Society
Finnish Mathematical Society
French Mathematical Society
Deutsche Mathematiker Vereinigung
Georgian Mathematical Union
Greek Mathematical Society
János Bolyai Mathematical Society, Hungary
Iceland Mathematical Society
Irish Mathematical Society
Italian Mathematical Society
Luxembourg Mathematical Society
Wiskundig Genootschap, The Netherlands
Norwegian Mathematical Society
Polish Mathematical Society
Portuguese Mathematical Society
Romanian Mathematical Society
Edinburgh Mathematical Society
Swedish Mathematical Society
Swiss Mathematical Society
Spanish Mathematical Society
Moscow Mathematical Society
Union of the Societies of Mathematicians,
    Physicists & Astronomers of Yugoslavia
Estonian Mathematical Society
Lithuanian Mathematical Society
S.M.A.I.
G.A.M.M.
I.M.A.

Acquisitions
and the South African Experience

Digby Sales

INTRODUCTION

The southern tip of Africa was colonized by the Dutch in 1652 and it is they who introduced reading and printing to the Cape of Good Hope. However, it was only in the 19th century under the influence of the British who had annexed the Cape in 1806 that publishing and bookselling spread. The details of this development can be found in ASC Hooper's contribution on this topic in the *Encyclopaedia of Publishing and the Book Arts* (New York 1994).

As background I wish to mention two factors which affect the present state of publishing and bookselling in South Africa, viz. censorship and education.

Censorship, particularly political censorship, had a profound effect on the free flow of information between 1965 and 1990. The Internal Security Act of 1976 (previously the Suppression of Communism Act of 1950) and the Publications Act of 1974 (previously the Publications and Entertainment Act of 1963) were the two most important pieces of legislation in this regard. Furthermore, the Publications Act controlled literature and to a certain extent religious writings. Films and theater also fell under its ambit. As a result of

---

Digby Sales is Acquisitions Librarian at the University of Cape Town, Jagger Library, Rondebosch 7700, South Africa.

[Haworth co-indexing entry note]: "Acquisitions and the South African Experience." Sales, Digby. Co-published simultaneously in *Collection Management* (The Haworth Press, Inc.) Vol. 19, Nos. 3/4, 1995, pp. 141-150; and: *Practical Issues in Collection Development and Collection Access: The 1993 Charleston Conference* (ed: Katina Strauch et al.) The Haworth Press, Inc., 1995, pp. 141-150. Multiple copies of this article/chapter may be purchased from The Haworth Document Delivery Center [1-800-3-HAWORTH; 9:00 a.m. - 5:00 p.m. (EST)].

© 1995 by The Haworth Press, Inc. All rights reserved.
141

this censorship there are gaps in South African library collections from this period.

There are 19 separate education departments due to the ethnic engineering of apartheid. This is for a population of just under 40 million people. The quality of the education has varied with the white sector being favored. This has resulted in a high drop-out rate among other sectors of the population with resulting illiteracy estimated between 9 and 15 million of the population.

LOCAL PUBLISHING

As an indication of the extent of local publishing the 1992 figures are given as supplied by the South African National Bibliography.

Out of a total of 7,717 items published, 5,729 were books and 1,988 were pamphlets. Only 4,203 were first editions (2,680 being books). Two interesting categories are the school books, 1,841, nearly a quarter of the production and the government publications, 418, which reflect the fragmentation of the country due to apartheid created structures (Table 1).

In 1992, 80% of the market share of the sale of publications was of educational books compared, for example, to 30% in the United Kingdom. Educational publishing is dominated by Afrikaaner owned firms with the major publishers in this field being Educum, De Jager-HAUM, Shooter and Shuter, Juta and Maskew Miller Longman. The last one being one of the four multinational publishing houses involved in South African educational publishing. The other three are Oxford University Press, MacMillan and Lexicon (the McGraw-Hill disinvested company).

Further information on the state of education publishing in South Africa can be found in recently published conference papers entitled *Publishing for Democratic Education* (Johannesburg: SACHED, 1993).

The multinational publishing companies are to a greater or lesser extent involved in general publishing. Butterworths together with Juta are the major legal publishers. The university presses of Natal, the Witwatersrand and Cape Town are relatively small and it has been general publishers that have provided reading matter for the local market. The main Afrikaans publishers are Tafelberg and

Human and Rossouw. There are a variety of local English language publishers such as Struik, Donker, Southern, David Philip, Ravan and Skotaville. It was particularly the last three who during the apartheid era risked ruin by publishing works relevant to the times and subsequently having some books banned.

THE BOOKTRADE

The bigger cities such as Cape Town, Durban, Johannesburg, Pretoria and Bloemfontein have a variety of bookshops, but on the whole bookselling is dominated by the Central News Agency which has shops in most towns of any size. It is very much a general store which sells stationery, toys, films, recorded music, magazines and books.

In the bigger cities bookshop chain stores such as Juta, Exclusive and van Schaik have branches. Academic bookselling is dominated by the Mast group of shops.

Local library supply is provided by the chains as well as by independent suppliers such as Fons Libris, Books etc., and Executive. Two of the specialist Africana shops, Clarke's and Thorolds, also do library supply. Within the country other types of specialties such as children, stamps and socialism can be found.

The high level of illiteracy and the shortage of disposal income have meant that some bookshops in the cities regard library supply as an important part of their business. As all but 10 of the 670 public libraries are served by one of the four provincial library services, these four have an inordinate influence on the booktrade (and also on selection).

An interesting phenomenon is the second-hand bookshop which is often also a swop-shop. This has been one way people have found to deal with the shortage of money and the high costs of books.

ACQUISITIONS LIBRARIANSHIP

This section reflects to a large extent my personal experiences and I shall be using the University of Cape Town Libraries to illustrate this aspect of the profession.

A separate library to serve the University of Cape Town was established in 1905. The present stock (1992) was 545,501 book volumes and 7,367 current periodical titles. The student population is 14,595 and the library staff has a complement of 205, of which 59 are qualified librarians. The materials budget for 1993 was R5 137 430 ($1,500,000); R3 497 456 ($1,020,000) has been set aside for periodicals, and the remaining R1 639 974 ($480,000) is being used to buy books and other materials such as video cassettes and music scores.

The Acquisitions Department consists of seven staff, two of whom are qualified librarians. Selection is largely done by the academics. The orders are processed through the Acquisitions Department where a large range of bibliographic tools are kept including the CD-ROMs, Whitaker's *Bookbank* and Bowker's *Books in Print Plus*. The orders are input into an in-house networked DBase III Plus system. As the library is linked to the Internet, orders are sent, where possible, by electronic mail in ASCII format to our overseas suppliers.

The numbers of orders and accessions for 1991 and 1992 and the source of the material by country in 1992 are as follows:

	1992	*1991*
Orders placed	12,809	10,500
Purchases accessioned	11,586	9,981
Donations accessioned	3,717	4,378

26.5% originated from Southern Africa
33.1% originated from North America
30.4% originated from the United Kingdom
10% originated from the rest of the world (mainly Europe)

Factors that have affected the supply of material to South African libraries have been censorship, sanctions, geographic isolation from

TABLE 1

PUBLISHING STATISTICS: 1992

Books	5,729
Pamphlets	1,988
Total	7,717

- 4,203 First Editions
- 1,841 School books
- 418 Government publications

the main publishers, and overseas publishers closing the market to direct importing (Table 2).

The effect of censorship was that libraries became involved in a lot of red tape as academic and research institutions are allowed to hold banned material in locked cupboards. The more profound influence was that certain views were not available leading to a general narrowness of outlook.

The effect of sanctions on library supply was largely to increase costs as the international library suppliers and subscription agents were able to obtain any material required, but often resulting in extra cost. For example UMI theses which at present cost us $55, we had to pay $72 via an intermediary until UMI once more started doing business with South Africa in May 1993. A further serious consequence of sanctions was that the value of the rand dropped. A table indicating this is attached showing the fall since 1988 (Table 3).

TABLE 2

FACTORS AFFECTING SUPPLY

Censorship and Sanctions

Geographic Isolation

Closed Market

TABLE 3

RAND/POUND EXCHANGE RATE
1988-1993

Pounds

0.29 0.27 0.25 0.23 0.21 0.19 0.17

JAN FEB MAR APR MAY JUN JUL AUG SEP OCT NOV DEC
— 1988   1989   -- 1990   —— 1991   —*— 1992   —⊕— 1993

RAND/DOLLAR EXCHANGE RATE
1988-1993

Dollars

0.48 0.43 0.38 0.33 0.28

JAN FEB MAR APR MAY JUN JUL AUG SEP OCT NOV DEC
— 1988   1989   -- 1990   —— 1991   —*— 1992   —⊕— 1993

TABLE 3 (continued)

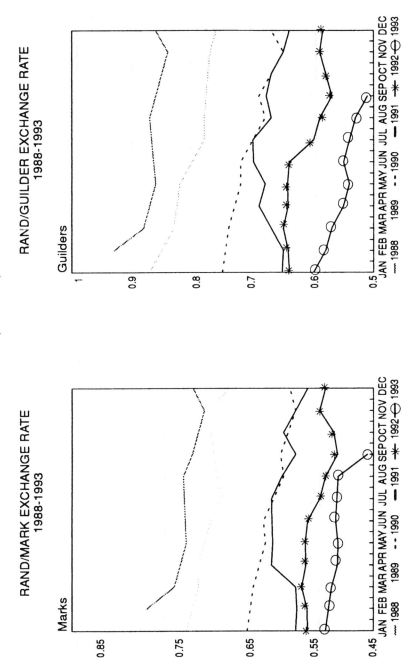

RAND/MARK EXCHANGE RATE
1988-1993

RAND/GUILDER EXCHANGE RATE
1988-1993

In this period the rand decreased against the dollar by 39% and the pound by 32%. This is reflected in the 75% increase in price of UCT's journals, whereas the number of titles increased by only 12%. In contrast the book prices increased by much less, 21%.

South Africa's distance from Europe and North America has meant that the delivery times for material were slow. For example up to two years ago it was taking on average 5-6 months for books to arrive from North America. From the United Kingdom it was taking 2-3 months. However, with the introduction of an airfreight service from the main library suppliers this has been halved and further helped by sending the orders electronically.

Publishing rights for South Africa fall into the British area and some British publishers have set the price for the South African market higher than a straight conversion. Booksellers, to cover their import costs, also add a larger factor than a straight conversion. In addition there is a 14% value added tax on books.

American publications have to come via Britain and therefore libraries have to pay the export price. For example Bowker's *Books in Print* is supplied by Butterworths in South Africa via their London office as they are Bowker's agent in South Africa.

FUTURE TRENDS IN PUBLISHING AND BOOKSELLING

I shall just pick out a few trends affecting South African libraries in the future.

There has been a healthy growth in publishing since the unbanning of the African National Congress and other liberation groups. However, there is a recession and the future redistribution of wealth is unlikely to result in much disposal income. Some publishers are therefore likely to go bankrupt. The growth area will be in educational publishing as a future government tries to improve the educational level of the youth.

The unbanning of the various liberation groups has resulted in there being no longer political censorship. Moral censorship is limited to a large extent to hard and soft pornography and to a certain extent homosexuality. Moral censorship is to a large extent determined by the tolerance level of society for this type of material however, political censorship is likely to return in areas such as racism and inciting people to violence, especially as these laws have not been repealed. It will be up to those who value the free flow of information to oppose any new censorship. This is where international support will be just as important as in the past.

Reintegration in the world community will make the Acquisitions Librarian's task easier in acquiring materials. There will be more competition by international library suppliers and the use of electronic media will speed up communication and supply. The only problem is that there will not be much money for library materials, especially books, as periodical prices are rising at a rate much faster than inflation.

In summary then the dominance of educational publishing is likely to continue except that the Afrikaaner publishers are unlikely to be the leaders in the field as in the past.

The growth of the booktrade will depend on increased literacy and wealth, especially as libraries are likely to have less money. The growth of library collections is likely to be slow and a trend particularly in the tertiary area is likely to be towards cooperative consortia.

APPENDIX 1

NON-EDUCATIONAL PUBLISHERS:

Butterworths
Human and Roussouw
Tafelberg
David Philip
Ravan
Skotaville
Jonathan Ball
AD. Donker
Southern Book Publishers
Struik
University Presses from:
  Witwatersrand
  Natal
  Cape Town

CHAIN STORES:

Central News Agency
Mast
Exclusive
Juta
Van Schaik

INDEPENDENTS:

Fons Libris
Executive
Books etc.
Clarke's
Thorold's
Phambili Books

Deselection of Serials:
The Chalmers University
of Technology Library Method

Rolf Hasslöw
Annika Sverrung

SUMMARY. In the fall of 1992 the Swedish government decided to let their currency float freely against all other currencies. This action caused serious problems for the Swedish academic libraries as they import most of their literature. Chalmers University of Technology Library purchases 96% of its journals and serials from outside Sweden. To cope with this new situation with some 25-30% less money to maintain the collections, a deselection process started, in which different methods were analyzed and tested. This led to a new method developed by Chalmers library for the deselection of journals. In this article, two methods, ICR (Institutional Cost Ratio) and CPU (Cost Per Use) developed in USA and Canada will be described and analyzed. The new Chalmers library method, in which the journals are allocated in proportion to the various Schools of Engineering and Architecture, and deselection carried out by means of quartiles and usage will be described.

CHALMERS UNIVERSITY OF TECHNOLOGY, SWEDEN: A BACKGROUND

Chalmers University of Technology (Chalmers) is located in Göteborg on the Swedish West Coast and is one of the Universities

Rolf Hasslöw and Annika Sverrung are affiliated with Chalmers University, The Library, S-412 96, Göteborg, Sweden.

[Haworth co-indexing entry note]: "Deselection of Serials: The Chalmers University of Technology Library Method." Hasslöw, Rolf, and Annika Sverrung. Co-published simultaneously in *Collection Management* (The Haworth Press, Inc.) Vol. 19, Nos. 3/4, 1995, pp. 151-170; and: *Practical Issues in Collection Development and Collection Access: The 1993 Charleston Conference* (ed: Katina Strauch et al.) The Haworth Press, Inc., 1995, pp. 151-170. Multiple copies of this article/chapter may be purchased from The Haworth Document Delivery Center [1-800-3-HAWORTH; 9:00 a.m. - 5:00 p.m. (EST)].

© 1995 by The Haworth Press, Inc. All rights reserved.

151

of Technology in Sweden. Chalmers consists of nine Schools of Engineering and Architecture: Mathematical and Computing Sciences, Physics and Engineering Physics, Chemical Engineering, Electrical and Computer Engineering, Mechanical and Vehicular Engineering, Civil Engineering, Architecture, Technology Management and Economics and Environmental Sciences. Approximately 100 departments at Chalmers are grouped into these schools of engineering and some departments have subdivisions. There are 4,200 full time students in the M.Eng programs (4 to 5 years). Some 750 M.Eng degrees are awarded every year, and 850 students follow the PhD programs, with some 150 PhDs awarded every year (including Licentiates comprising approximately 4 years of study above the M.Eng level). Chalmers has 500 faculty members and 1,900 employees (full time equivalents). The annual turnover is 143 million ECU (90/91), where 69% goes towards research and PhD programs and 31% to undergraduate and Masters programs. There is one Faculty (Engineering which includes Physical Science) in close cooperation with the Faculty of Physical Science of the University of Göteborg.

There is also one associated self-governing college–The College of Applied Engineering and Maritime Studies, with approximately 1,500 students in the 2-3 year program.[1]

CHALMERS LIBRARY

Chalmers library contains some 90,000 book volumes and 4,000 current serial titles. Out of these serial titles, 1,900 are purchased journal subscriptions, 420 titles are on a standing order basis and the remaining 1,700 titles are acquired through exchange agreements or received as gifts. Approximately 85% of the acquisitions budget is dedicated to maintaining subscriptions and standing orders. The collection from the last ten years is available via open access.

Our serial collection is not available for loan. Photocopying facilities are provided at cost price. The library policy is that the journals should always be accessible on site for the users. The library is open not only for university staff and students, but also for industrial users and general public. The total acquisitions budget for literature is approximately $950,000 per year.

The journals purchased by the library originate from the following countries:

USA	35.6%
England	30.3%
Germany	13.5%
The Netherlands	12.6%
Sweden	4.0%
Other	4.0%

COLLECTION DEVELOPMENT AT CHALMERS UNIVERSITY OF TECHNOLOGY LIBRARY

BIBSAM (The Swedish Royal Library's Office for National Planning and Coordination) has taken an interest in questions concerning acquisitions and acquisition policy. They have suggested acquisition guidelines, mainly based on American models for Swedish academic libraries. Collection development means building up a library collection both qualitatively and quantitatively. It includes developing an acquisition policy, establishing plans for selection methods as well as measuring user needs and evaluating existing collections (Just-in-Case, Just-in-Time, or the famous Swedish model, Somewhere-in-Between). Furthermore, collection development includes coordination of selection, shelving, storing and weeding. Cooperation with library users is also very important. This is a planning and decision process that concerns and influences not only the library, but the whole university.

Shrinking budgets, rising costs for literature, less storage space combined with new techniques such as electronic communication and electronic document delivery may force libraries to reconsider their acquisition policies. One model that BIBSAM recommends when deciding on the collection development policy is ALA's (American Library Association) model, that can be briefly described with the following levels:

A. *Comprehensive level*: the collections have everything on the topic no matter what the language, age, level or format.

B. *Research level*: libraries support the acquisition of major published source materials required for dissertations and independent research. It includes specialized reference tools, conference proceedings, professional society publications, multiple editions, bibliographies, important foreign language material and at least 65% of available periodical titles. Older and superseded materials must be retained for historical research.

C. *Instructional support level*: describes a collection that sufficiently supports undergraduate, independent and most graduate level instruction but not postgraduate level research. Complete collections of important writers, basic bibliographies, major reference works and selected works of secondary writers should be in the collection.

D. *Basic information level*: suggests very selective choices at the introductory subject level, reference works, journals and other materials. These collections are not sufficiently intensive to support courses for independent and senior level research in the subject area.

E. *Minimal level*: this level is assigned when very basic works support user's needs.

F. *Out-of-scope level*: suggests that the institution does not have an interest or mission in a specific subject area and the library therefore should not support acquisitions in that subject.[2]

Chalmers library has up till now had the ambition to acquire literature according to level B. When the Swedish government in late 1992 decided to let the Swedish Crown float freely against other currencies, this had considerable negative consequences for the library's budget planning. When we analyzed the situation during Spring 1993 for the next year's subscriptions we calculated that we would lose about 20-25% against the major currencies. If we estimated the nominal price increases as approximately 10%, this would mean that our acquisitions budget needed to be strengthened with about 30-35%. Previously the library has been compensated for price increases with 3-7%, less the nominal price increases. In this situation, and taking account of new technology, new and faster channels for document delivery and the depreciation of the Swedish Crown, we had to radically reconsider our acquisition policy.

With the library's current collection intensity we had managed to reach level B for approximately 75-80% of the university's different departments and research programs. In the future we will probably have to lower our ambition for our research support. Maybe this is sufficient, if we can efficiently manage to supply the desired literature through other channels.[3,4]

PLAN OF ACTION

We decided to prepare a proposal for subscription cancellations for approximately $250,000. We also decided to investigate different methods for evaluation and deselection processes. These activities would be combined with intense lobbying towards the President and the Faculty members to make them understand the gravity of the situation. We also acted at a national level. In cooperation with the Technological University Libraries in Sweden, we informed the Minister of Education about the situation.

The practical work with the cancellation process was carried out by the Head of Technical Services Department and the Acquisitions Librarian. The negotiation with the President and the Faculty was undertaken by the Chief Librarian who also informed them about our collection intensity and the library's desired collection intensity, in combination with other literature delivery methods.

METHODS FOR DESELECTION

In this section we will describe the different methods used for our deselection process. The main criterion was to try to suggest a method that would mean less negative consequences for our customers while at the same time living up to our ambition to remain on level B for the majority of the university departments.

User Evaluation Study

Chalmers library was fortunate to have a rather recent user evaluation study of the journal collection. The purpose of that study was to find out to what degree our journal collection was used. Primarily we were interested in the non-use and low-frequency-use of the journals.

Of the above mentioned 4,000 journals, the use of about 3,000 journals, or 75% of our holdings, were measured during autumn 1989 to spring 1990.

The number of journals measured 1989/90, sorted by LC classmark, is shown below.

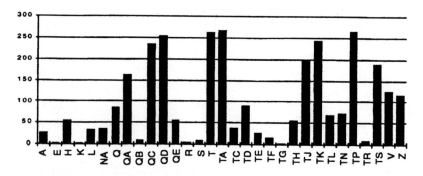

Out of these 3,000 journals, 1,750 were purchased journals and the rest were gifts and exchange journals. We limited the study to journals that were available via open access. For Chalmers library that means journals published during the last ten years. We excluded the reference collection and the monograph series. We also excluded the journals in library science and in librarianship, which we later evaluated in a separate study. Information about the survey and notices requesting our customers not to reshelve used material were posted in strategic places in user area. All journal issues that were used during this period were recorded on the computer print out of our periodical holdings. The recording also included journals used for interlibrary loan.

Criteria and Misleading Information

Certain criteria were stipulated before conducting the survey. It is difficult to calculate the use of a collection when part of the journal collection is in bound volumes. We could not know if the user had consulted one or more issues of that journal. We decided to register the bound volumes as one use. At Chalmers we bind few journals, issues are stored in boxes. About the same problem occurred when the whole box was removed from the shelf. We decided to register that as one use as well. But if, let's say three issues were taken out from one box, this was registered as three uses. Where to draw the line in order to receive an objective survey is hard to decide. We had to let the persons involved in the recording work make their own decisions in some cases. One must take into consideration that a survey of this kind contains several sources of error that can give misleading results. Many of the issues were probably reshelved by the users. We noted for example that one person with a favorite journal came every day to use this journal so that he could be sure that it would not be canceled.

The result of this survey was that, after a supplementary consultation with the departments, only a few journals were withdrawn. Many of the faculty members who did not use the journal during the time of the survey claimed that the journal did have a value for them and that they wanted the library to retain it. So the final result, was that only 192 titles were withdrawn in 1990, out of which 109 were gifts or titles received on an exchange basis.

The remaining journal collection was used as basis three years later, in 1992/93, when we decided to make a deselection plan.

Preliminary Work for the Deselection Plan

The result of the user survey had been entered into FileMaker, a database program, on a Macintosh computer. But testing different methods of doing calculations on the material we found that the FileMaker program was not sufficient for our purposes. We have, however, had good experience of calculations based on the Excel program, so the file was converted into Excel and we started the clerical work of entering data into the computer. This data included, among other things, the identification of the different methods of acquisition such as subscription, package plans, gifts and acquisition on exchange basis for each journal in the file. For example, single titles included in subscription packages were listed separately. Finally the actual 1993 subscription price was entered for each title. During this last process we did not take into consideration possible discounts such as package plan subscription or early payment reductions, etc.

After evaluating different methods of deselection by reading articles on the subject we considered two different methods as being the most interesting and appropriate for our purpose. The methods we considered interesting for us were "Institutional Cost Ratio" (ICR) developed at The Biomedical Library at Lawrence Livermore National Laboratory, and "Cost per Use" (CPU) developed at Queen Elizabeth II Library, Memorial University of Newfoundland, Canada.[6]

Institutional Cost Ratio (ICR)

R. K. Hunt at the Biomedical Library at Lawrence Livermore National Laboratory (LLNL)[7] has developed a mathematical formula that provides a measure of the cost-effectiveness of subscribing to a journal. This formula provides a comparison between the cost of owning a journal with the cost of acquiring individual articles through the interlibrary loan system (ILL).

The costs that were taken into consideration were subscription costs, interlibrary loan costs, cost of staff, and shelving and storage costs. These costs were estimated in combination with the level of use to determine the institutional cost ratio (ICR). By comparing all cost aspects, the library could logically choose the most cost-effective alternative for each title.

The formula is based on three variables and three constants:

$$ICR = (U*I)/[P + M + (L*S)]$$

U = Annual use
P = Annual subscription cost
L = Size of bound collection
I = Cost of performing an ILL
M = Annual cost of maintaining a subscription
S = Shelving and storage cost

The three constants I, M, and S were established as $17.20 for an ILL transaction, $27.00 per title for subscription maintenance, and $6.00 per linear foot for shelving and storage cost.

We found it interesting to test this formula on our holdings at Chalmers. With this formula the cost-effectiveness for the *Journal of Applied Physics* would be:

$$(105*17.20)/[1680 + 27 + (15*6.00)] = 1.01$$

Figures over 1.0 for a given journal are considered cost-effective for the library to hold. This particulate journal in the example comes only just over the line even if it has 105 registered uses during a period of one year. When using this mathematical formula on the collections at Chalmers it appears that 74.4% of our journals got a lower ranking than 1.0. The comparable figures for LLNL were 61.4%. For Chalmers, this would mean that a bit over 1,200 titles should be cancelled. These journals comprised almost 43% of the total use determined by the survey conducted in 89/90.

LLNL circulated a list over their low ranked titles and if five or more persons claimed that they wanted a journal the library decided to keep it. At Chalmers library, when we looked at the results of the journal use, those with 5 or more registered uses (not necessarily 5 different users), we found that, if we applied the LLNL formula, we should cancel 38% of the titles. These journals, however show a significantly lower usage and they only comprise 4.4% of the total use.

The advantage of this method is that it provides figures that show the actual cost for maintaining a journal subscription, as compared with ILL.

The disadvantage is that this does not take into account the large fluctuations in currency rates which influence the ICR. When comparing ICR before the depreciation of the Swedish Crown, the result would have been that 70% of the journals got a lower ranking than 1.0, comprising 38% of total use. It is also difficult to compare our bound collections with collections consisting of unbound issues. The figures for Chalmers library can also be misleading because we have not analyzed our exact costs for ILL, shelving, storing and maintaining journal subscriptions. Furthermore, the method does not take into account the quality aspects of the information provided by a specific journal. Livermore decided that even if the ICR was low, a journal which five or more persons explicitly wanted to retain was worth keeping. At Chalmers we are not sure at what level we should set the limit for keeping a journal. We concluded that this method would not be so useful for our long term collection planning policy. It is, however, an interesting method, one of several for evaluation of serial collections, and we will later make use of this as a part of what we call the Chalmers library model.

Cost Per Use (CPU)

Milne and Tiffany at the Queen Elizabeth II Library, Memorial University of Newfoundland, St. John's, Newfoundland, Canada[8] have used a similar method for evaluating their serials. They also compared the cost of subscribing to a serial with the cost of providing interlibrary loans. The factors in the mathematical formula used to determine the cost effectiveness were:

$$\frac{\text{COST}}{\text{USE}}$$

COST equals the current subscription price for a serial.
USE is A*B*C where:

A equals the total number of registered use during a one year period.

B equals the adjustment factor for underrecording of use, in the study 3/2.

C equals the adjustment factor for the number of years of issues surveyed in the study. Here they used an adjustment factor called CPC (Cumulative Percentage of Citations) based on data from ISI (Institute of Scientific Information).

D Chalmers had to add one extra adjustment factor D, so that our survey corresponded to a whole year. Our factor D equals 1.25.

At Chalmers library use of the last ten years issues of journals were measured (we did not take into consideration if we had a full ten years period for each title). Our adjustment factor for C, then became 100/68.

The formula for the *Journal of Applied Physics* then reads:

$$\frac{1680}{84*1.5*1.47*1.25} = \frac{1680}{231.5} = 7.26$$

This figure can then be compared with the library's actual cost for ILL costs for that journal for a year. Figures lower than 28 are considered cost-effective for a library to hold. The advantage with this method is that it not only considers the actual use of a journal, but also combines it with the subscription price. Using this method it is easy for the library to decide when a journal is cost effective or when it would be worthwhile to cancel journal subscriptions. The disadvantage is that a journal with rather high registered use in combination with high price appears to be cost ineffective compared with journals with low price and low frequency of use. For Chalmers library this formula would, for example, show that we ought to cancel the journal "Ferroelectrics" with 41 registered use occasions and keep the journal "Physics Teacher" with only two registered use occasions. So if we don't take into account the quality aspects (or demanded information sources), but use this method strictly it would result in some peculiar collection effects. It could also be difficult to defend this policy against the faculty. This method also favors research groups with many members as they potentially have greater need to consult one and the same journal.

Conclusions, Leading to a New Model– The Chalmers Library Model

The ICR-method states that a journal is cost-effective at an ICR of 1.0 or more, and the CPU-method estimates that a journal is cost-effective receiving a CPU $28 or less. When comparing these two methods on the Chalmers library collections we obtained quite different results. The highest measured CPU with an ICR at 1.0 is only $ 7.95, which should mean that only 5.8% of our journals were cost-effective. On the other hand, a CPU of $28 sets the limit already at an ICR of 0.26 which means that 64.2% of our journals are cost-effective. The differences shown between the two methods, when comparing the respective results, shows such large discrepancies that it was difficult for us to make any decisions from the results obtained. We decided, therefore, to develop a new method for the deselection plan–the Chalmers library model.

In the Swedish language we have a word "lagom" that lacks an equivalent in other languages. The meaning of this word is not too much and not too little but rather something or somewhere in between.

When deciding which model to use for our deselection plan, we created a model "somewhere in between." We tested two new models which had their origins in both of the above described methods.

The Less Frequented Journals

This method is strictly based upon our user survey. It basically says that the less frequently used journals should be cancelled. For Chalmers library, aiming for a $250,000 cut in the acquisitions budget, we would have to cancel approximately 930 journals or almost 25% of our total journal/serial collection. Expressed in another way this would mean that 40% of our purchased journals/serials would be cancelled. This method would surely force us to keep only what is really heavily demanded at present. The disadvantage is that some of the subject fields would be totally erased from our collections. For some departments at the university we would only reach level F according to the ALA, or the recommendations by BIBSAM at the Swedish Royal Library. This discrepancy between library acquisition policy and the need for a deselection, we decided was not acceptable. Another critical factor using this method is the limited period during which the user survey was conducted. The needs for information of the research workers and students depends on the subjects and the point they are at in the research process. User needs for information can occur irregularly, and when this happens, several backvolumes will have to be consulted, as for example when writing an article. So we also consider this method to be somewhat limited and unfair. This method, however, served as an additional platform for our next and final method.

Deselection by Subject Through Median and Quartiles

When using this method, our main intention was to create a deselection plan that would affect our users as little as possible. Our effort is still to serve them in the best possible way. This new method was also based upon the user survey, but now the gifts and journals received on an exchange basis were removed from the survey method. We only evaluated the purchased journals and serials. We divided them into sections equivalent with the shelving system used by the library. Our classmarks originate from Library of Congress and we have 31 main subject categories. After sorting the journals into these categories we rearranged them according to the subjects of the nine Schools of Engineering and Architecture. The number of journals sorted by classmark is shown below:

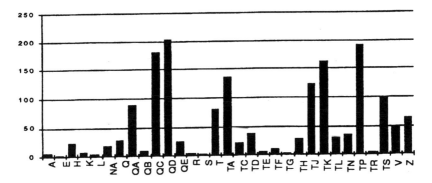

When arranged according to the subjects of the nine Schools of Engineering and Architecture, the number of journals appeared as follows:

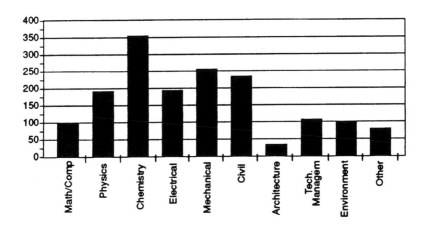

The middle value of a statistical population is called median. One can also locate a value one-quarter of the way through ranking and a value three-quarters of the way through ranking. When a list, as in our case, was listed by School and registering use from low to high, these quarters are called the first and the third quartile.

Ranking low to high.

First quartile	$(n + 1)/4$
Median	$(n + 1)/2$
Third quartile	$3(n + 1)/4$

Each category of periodicals was then divided into quartiles. Doing this we could easily estimate the level needed to conduct a deselection of journals. The advantage of this method is that the less frequent material within each subject area, sorted according to School can be cancelled. Just canceling the less 25% of journals for each School was not enough so we had to add some extra criteria to reach our level. If one cancels the less frequent journals according to the lower quartile, including all journals within the same frequency of use, and all journals with one or less registered use, this will give a more fair distribution per School of Engineering and Architecture. This method allows us to keep a higher level (maybe a little bit lower than present) for each School, according to the ALA's recommendations. According to this method, the deselected journals amounted to 495 titles representing a cost of approximately $150,000. The remaining sum of $100,000 is planned to come from cancellations of some of our expensive standing order series plus journals not cancelled according to the lower quartile but that have a Cost Per Use over 75. This action will give the total amount of $250,000. The total number of journals then becomes 576. Even this method has it is disadvantages. The major one is that the number of titles within each category varies a lot. So "small" subjects are reduced disproportionally heavily, though not so much as if we used some of the other methods.[9]

CONCLUSION

After presenting the figures, and describing the consequences for the University with respect to education and research, we gained support from the Faculty Board. They expressed their opinion that an economic compensation, due to the rising costs, must be considered. In their letter to the President they urged the importance of a high quality and international standard in the library's collections and that the library must continue to give good service to users in the future. Representatives from the regional, small universities and colleges in the West Swedish region also emphasized the great importance Chalmers library has for them. The Office of the President decided that the library was of crucial importance for the University and consequently they would compensate the library to a certain extent for the price increases. The library was guaranteed a 6% budget adjustment, due to normal price increases. Furthermore they decided on a compensation for the depreciation of the Swedish crown with an additional 14% and a guarantee of 11% for price increases during the next fiscal year due to future currency fluctuations. Further needs for coming years will be considered within the ordinary budget calculations.

To sum up we can state the fact that the library budget has increased 20%, which means that our cancellations will not be so extensive as we first calculated. About 300 journals will be canceled representing approximately a cost of $100,000.

REFERENCES

1. *Research at Chalmers University of Technology, Göteborg, Sweden 1992-1994.* Anna Bergius (ed). Chalmers University of Technology. Göteborg 1992.
2. R J Wood and K Strauch. *Collection Assessment: A Look at the RLG Conspectus.* The Haworth Press, Inc. New York. 1992.
3. H Rinne Mendes. *Beståndsutveckling eller förvärvspolitik?* Tidskrift för dokumentation 42, no 3, 1986, p. 61-67.
4. G E Gorman and B R Howes. *Collection Development for Libraries.* Bowker-Saur. London. 1989.
5. A Sverrung. *Användarundersökning på CTHB 1989-1990.* Internal Report at Chalmers University of Technology Library Göteborg, 1993.
6. T E Nisonger. *Collection Evaluation in Academic Libraries: A Literature Guide and Annotated Bibliography.* Libraries Unlimited Inc. Engelwood CO. 1992.
7. R K Hunt. *Journal deselection in a biomedical research library: A mediated mathematical approach.* Bulletin of Medical Library Association 78, no. 1 (Jan. 1990) 45-48.
8. D Milne and B Tiffany. *A survey of the cost-effectiveness of serials: A cost-per-use method.* Serials Librarian 19 nos 3/4. 1991, p. 137-149.
9. W S Peters. *Counting for Something: Statistical Principles and Personalia.* Springer Verlag. New York. 1987.

Note: The currency rates used are from March 1, 1993.

USD	7.84	DEM	4.75
GBP	11.26	NLG	4.23

APPENDIX

Deselection of Journals
at Chalmers University of Technology
Library
1993/94

The Library   4,000   serial titles
                 1,850   purchased
                   420   standing orders
                 1,730   exchange or gifts

The expenditure for the fiscal year 1992/93 was $ 900,000 (purchased journals, standing orders and CD-ROM).

Institutional Cost Ratio (ICR)

Developed by:

The Biomedical Library at Lawrence Livermore National Laboratory, USA.

$$ICR = (U^*I) / [P + M(L^*S)]$$

U = Annual use
P = Annual subscription cost
L = Size of bound collection
       (measured)
I = Cost of performing an ILL
M = Annual cost of maintaining a subscription
S = Shelving and storage cost

The three constants I, M and S were established as:

I = USD 17.20
M = USD 27.00
S = USD   6.00 /per linear foot

The ICR for the *Journal of Applied Physics* would be

$(105*17.20) / [1680 + 27 + (15*6)] = 1.01$

Figures over 1.0 are considered cost-effective.

According to this method 74.4% of our purchased journals got a lower ranking than 1.0.

These journals comprised 43% of the total use.

Cost-Per-Use (CPU)

Developed by:

Queen Elizabeth II Library, Memorial University of Newfoundland, Canada.

$$CPU = \frac{Cost}{Use}$$

Cost = Annual subscription cost

Use = A*B*C*D

A = Annual use
B = Adjustment factor for underrecording, 3/2
C = Adjustment factor for surveyed issues, 100/68
D = Adjustment factor for correspond to a whole year, 1.25

$$\frac{COST}{A*1.5*1.47*1.25}$$

The CPU for the *Journal of Applied Physics* then reads:

$$\frac{1680}{84 \times 1.5 \times 1.47 \times 1.25} = \frac{1680}{231.5} = 7.26$$

The CPU method estimates that a journal is cost-effective receiving a CPU $ 28 or less.

According to this method we should cancel 35.8% of our purchased journal collection.

These journals comprised 4.1% of the total use.

Different methods that provide a measure of the collections.

*User evaluation study 1989/90

*Remaining 1,660 purchased journals

*Institutional Cost Ratio (ICR)

*Cost-Per-Use (CPU)

*Deselection by subject through quartiles

The average currency rates, Fall 1992 (Aug. Sep. Oct.) compared with the same period, Fall 1993.

	Fall 1992	*Fall 1993*	*Change*
USD	5.30	8.19	+ 54.5%
GBP	9.93	12.20	+ 22.9%
DEM	3.69	4.81	+ 30.4%
NLG	3.27	4.28	+ 30.9%
Other			approx. + 30.0%

How to Use Your Money Best

(1) Cancel journal subscriptions—25-30% are never used.

(2) Cancel your standing orders, buy single titles when demanded. Up to 40% are never used.

(3) Be more selective when purchasing books or starting new subscriptions.

(4) More cooperation—both on a National level and within your University.

(5) Keep an eye on the various price policies from publishers and vendors.

(6) If you do not have to, do not bind your collections.

(7) New media can save money, why subscribe to both print and CD. Cancel one of your copies.

Inside Information

* Access to bibliographic records from the British Library

* The 10,000 most requested journals

* Records from October 1992

* Updated two times a week

* Provides document delivery (March 1994)

* Searchable fields:
    (1) Word(s) in title
    (2) Author(s) name
    (3) Journal title
    (4) Volume title
    (5) Volume editor(s)

BookFind–CD

* Access to over 1.5 million English-language titles

* Over 2,000 subject classifications

* Several searchable fields

* Include full bibliographic details with abstracts and contents

* Produce lists for user selection

* Make the Library's stock collection more appropriate

Are the Methods Working?
Where Do We Go from Here?

Susan H. Zappen

SUMMARY. Subscription costs have troubled Rensselaer since 1988. The libraries have canceled 849 subscriptions since 1990. I have condensed what I have learned into the Ten Commandments for Serials Cancelations which instruct libraries to: educate and involve faculty; refrain from using book money or asking for more money; cancel the expensive titles; rely upon journal use studies; create small, focused lists; reward effort and cooperation; promote resource sharing; and foster communication. With a crystal ball, I look into the future to see: more resource sharing; more electronic exchange of information; changes in the tenure system and in accreditation requirements; the demise of some journals and publishers; increased market share for society publishers; renewed interest in university publishing; and struggles with issues of ownership and copyright, with preservation of electronic information, and with the issue of free versus fee-based library information. I see a challenging future for all of us!

I like to relate to conference themes. Last year, in keeping with the Marshall McLuhan theme, I visually massaged you with calla lilies wrapped in black ribbon. The flowers were for our library journal collections that once were but are no more. This year, I thought about bringing in a big black cauldron with smoking dry

Susan H. Zappen is Acquisitions and Serials Librarian at Rensselaer Polytechnic Institute, Troy, NY 12180.

[Haworth co-indexing entry note]: "Are the Methods Working? Where Do We Go from Here?" Zappen, Susan H. Co-published simultaneously in *Collection Management* (The Haworth Press, Inc.) Vol. 19, Nos. 3/4, 1995, pp. 171-183; and: *Practical Issues in Collection Development and Collection Access: The 1993 Charleston Conference* (ed: Katina Strauch et al.) The Haworth Press, Inc., 1995, pp. 171-183. Multiple copies of this article/chapter may be purchased from The Haworth Document Delivery Center [1-800-3-HAWORTH; 9:00 a.m. - 5:00 p.m. (EST)].

© 1995 by The Haworth Press, Inc. All rights reserved.

ice. After all, we bubble and toil with serials cancellations. And they certainly cause us plenty of trouble. The cauldron wouldn't fit under the airplane seat in front of me. Instead, I brought my crystal ball to help us look ahead. It's not really crystal clear, but then neither is anything to do with serials.

Subscription costs that far exceed library resources have been a problem for Rensselaer since 1988. We have canceled 849 titles since 1990. We have lost at least 25% of our serials. What I have learned about the serials pricing crisis and serials cancellations, I have condensed into the Ten Commandments for Serials Cancellations (see Exhibit 1). I will talk about them with you before I bring out my crystal ball again for a look into the future.

THOU SHALT NOT STEAL BOOK MONEY

If your utility bill is too high, you don't give up food. You conduct an energy audit. You cut back on energy consumption. If your serial expenditures are too high, don't sacrifice books. In 1988 the Rensselaer Libraries froze book budgets to cover a $60,000 serials deficit. Big mistake. Our freeze coincided with a nearly 14% increase in the average cost of a new book.[1] The dip in Figure 1 shows clearly what happened to our book collection. The effects are lasting. There are titles that we should have, but never will obtain. Figure 2 depicts the erosion of our materials budget by rising subscription costs. We learned our lesson. We have established a cap on serials expenditures of 75%-80% of our materials budget to protect our ability to purchase books.

THOU SHALT NOT COVET THY UNIVERSITY'S MONEY

Money isn't the answer. Say it to university administrators only when they're sitting down. No one has ever said that to them before. Money isn't the answer. You may not yet believe it, but you will. Three years ago I didn't believe it. I learned it the hard way. Rensselaer Libraries initiated a serials cancellation project to cover the expected deficit in FY 1988-1989. Just before the cancellations

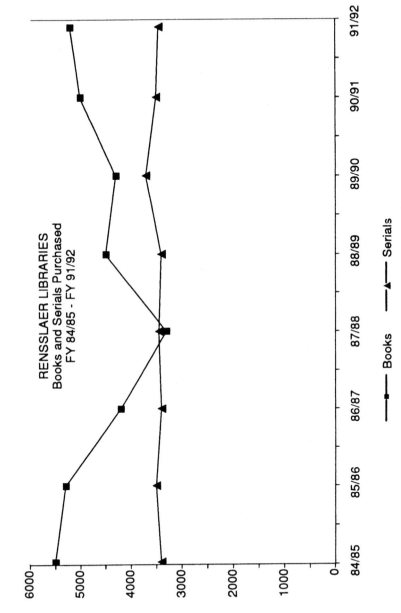

FIGURE 1

RENSSLAER LIBRARIES
Books and Serials Purchased
FY 84/85 - FY 91/92

173

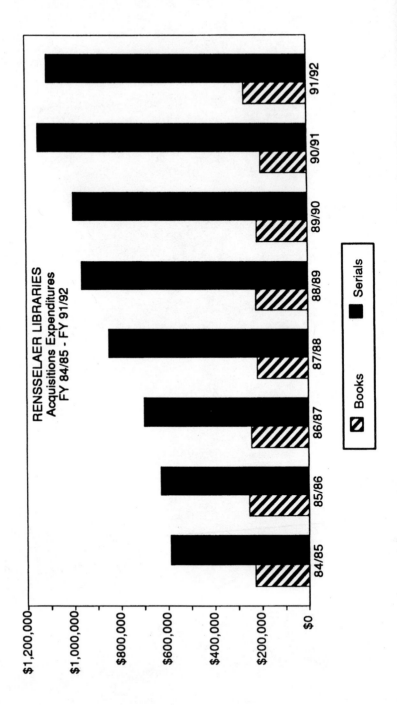

FIGURE 2

RENSSELAER LIBRARIES
Acquisitions Expenditures
FY 84/85 - FY 91/92

were finalized, the Institute provided additional funds. At last! Administrators with infinite wisdom who understood that libraries need more money. With more money our problems were solved. NOT! Even our generous budget for FY 1990-1991 was no match for the 22%-39% price increase of many STM titles. Some titles doubled and even tripled in price.

That's when I learned the most important lesson of all. Money is not the answer. No one library can keep up with both the rising costs of subscriptions and the proliferation of new serial titles. No one library can afford just in case acquisitions. Since 1990 serials cancellations have become a way of life for Rensselaer Libraries. And I have developed a new persona. I am now known as the "Serial Killer."

THOU SHALT EDUCATE FACULTY

Most faculty are unaware of library subscription costs and other information-cost issues. They haven't heard of differential pricing. Most equate copyright issues with the fluorescent green warnings we have taped to photocopy machines. Most have not considered the link between their tenure system which rewards and promotes quantity of publications and library problems with journal proliferation. Most believe that the problem with serials is a money problem with a money solution that the library better solve.

Until recently, most thought that renewals deficits and serials cancellations were problems unique to their university. Articles in *The Chronicle of Higher Education* and in professional publications have increased awareness of both the seriousness and the global nature of the problem. We have used information from the Association for Research Libraries about the declining purchasing power of libraries, information about serials cuts at major research libraries, along with information similar to what I have shown you in Figures 1 and 2 to educate our faculty. You may also discover, as I have, that colleagues in your library need to be educated as well.

Our library director also distributed The University of Minnesota's Senate Library Committee agenda for action. The agenda encourages faculty: to consolidate their research findings into one article rather than several; to become aware of cost issues; to consider whether or not scholarship is best served by relinquishing copyright of articles to commercial publishers; to encourage their professional associations to regularly evaluate their relationship with commercial publishers; and to stimulate discussion of the crisis in scholarly communication at their professional meetings.[2]

THOU SHALT INVOLVE FACULTY

It is simply good management to involve faculty. Involvement helps dispel the them-versus-us attitude. It helps create a cooperative atmosphere. We seek faculty input for collection development. We should seek it for serials cancellations. I have met a couple of librarians who have canceled serials on a large scale without faculty input. The one librarian, at a small college library, had no problem. The other librarian, at a community college library, was troubled by the lack of input. It was difficult for her to cancel titles because years of no budget increases had left her with very little to begin with. Each of Rensselaer's cancellation projects has involved faculty input. All faculty have been allowed to review cancellation lists and to suggest titles for cancellation. We provided journal lists grouped by school with prices both on our opac and on paper to encourage their involvement.

THOU SHALT NOT KILL THE INNOCENT TITLES

Cancel the expensive titles, the ones that dramatically increase in price, the ones that are causing your fiscal problems. Cancel the offending titles, not the $25 or $50 subscriptions which have not caused your fiscal problems and will not give you any long-term savings gain. This approach is one that university administrators can accept and appreciate. It shows common sense and good fiscal management. Bottom line people love it! If libraries had done this all along, we could have put a stop to the upward spiraling of costs and with it, the downward spiraling of subscriptions. My library would probably have 400-500 more serial titles on the shelf today if we had obeyed this commandment.

HONOR THY JOURNAL USE STUDIES

Rely upon journal use studies. As imperfect as they may be, they are accepted by faculty. Faculty do see the logic in canceling titles with little use and high subscription costs. Some do need more convincing than others. In June, at a NASIG workshop on journal use studies, I heard one librarian tell how she convinced a skeptical professor that the journal in question was not being used. For a year, serials staff stapled shut each issue as it arrived. At the end of the year, she showed the professor all the issues, still neatly stapled shut.

Our faculty accept the results of our use studies which go back about ten years. Our most recent use study is an on-going one which will help us with future cancellation projects. From this study we have identified 46 little-used, high-priced titles which may yet be canceled to keep us within budget during FY 1993-1994. Throughout all our cancellation projects, bibliographers expressed the concern that interlibrary loan requests generated by cancellations would drastically increase. It hasn't happened as you can see in Figure 3. We have steady growth, but we are not even averaging one request per canceled title. It makes me value use studies even more. It also makes me wonder if we haven't overrated the value of many of our journals.

REMEMBER TO USE SMALL FOCUSED LISTS

Rensselaer's approach to serials cancellations in each successive year has been evolutionary and incremental. Each year we have tried to improve upon what we did the year before. In our first approach we gave journal lists with prices to each school. We asked faculty to mark each title with "Cancel," "Keep," or "Maybe" (maybe meaning cancel if necessary). The lists were too long and too many faculty simply said "keep" to everything. If you use this approach, emphasize that you will cancel titles marked "maybe" and "keep" if there are an insufficient number of titles marked "cancel." Always include subscription costs on any list you create and distribute.

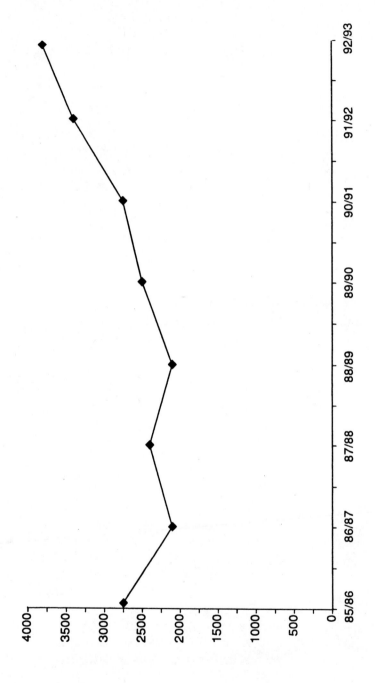

FIGURE 3. Journal Article Requests.

EXHIBIT 1

TEN COMMANDMENTS

FOR SERIALS CANCELLATIONS

Thou Shalt Not Steal Book Money

Thou Shalt Not Covet Thy University's Money

Thou Shalt Educate Faculty

Thou Shalt Involve Faculty

Thou Shalt Not Kill Innocent Titles

Honor Thy Journal Use Studies

Remember to Use Small, Focused Lists

Thou Shalt Reward Effort and Cooperation

Thou Shalt Promote Resource Sharing

Thou Shalt Foster Communication

We also used a core list approach. We asked faculty to identify 10 journals that are important for their individual research, 10 journals that are important to their general discipline, and 10 journals that are important for their teaching/course work. All responses were compiled into one core list for each school. Any title not on a core list became vulnerable to cancellation. Now we can focus faculty review of titles to the smaller list of non-core titles. The smaller list makes serials cancellations less overwhelming. Because faculty created the core lists, they can accept the cancellation of a non-core title with less emotion. Be prepared to revise your core list as programs and curricula change.

THOU SHALT REWARD EFFORT AND COOPERATION

Two of our schools took the core list approach very seriously. The Schools of Management and Architecture reviewed their serials thoroughly and canceled more titles than required in order to purchase new titles. It was a win-win situation. The libraries were able to cancel titles to reduce costs while the schools were able to order titles that meet their current research and teaching needs. In the process, the journal collection in those subject areas was evaluated, thinned, then revitalized. We continue to allow faculty to add a title at any time if they cancel a title of equal cost.

THOU SHALT PROMOTE RESOURCE SHARING

David Kohl, Dean and University Librarian of the University of Cincinnati, in the October 1 issue of *Library Journal,* calls the autonomous academic library trying to collect everything a dinosaur.[3] And we all know what happened to the dinosaurs. We can bemoan the fact that we are understaffed and underfunded, that we have not been given our fair share of the budget pie, or we can grow up. We face extinction or evolution. Traditionally, we have equated resource sharing with interlibrary loan. It's time to use the available technologies and seize the opportunities presented by cooperation among libraries to expand levels and kinds of access.

As we have canceled serials at Rensselaer, we have increased access. We added *Current Contents, Applied Science and Technology Index, EI Page One,* then various Wilson indexes to our opac. We have linked our holdings to the citations. Rensselaer patrons can generate electronic requests for materials, both those we own and those we don't own. After several months of negotiations, The State

University of New York at Albany (SUNYA) Library and The New York State Library are now using *Current Contents* on our opac. Eventually, we will add SUNYA and New York State Library holdings to *Current Contents* and offer electronic ILL ordering of articles among the libraries. We are also working on an online union list of serials of the three institutions which will make it easy for patrons to see who owns what.

We are providing what we call a "Connect" service. By simply choosing a number from the Connect menu, users are automatically connected through the Internet to the systems of 17 other universities. Free access to Carl Uncover presents new possibilities which we need to explore. Do we make it available on our opac? Or do we link it to our ILL process? As we started canceling journals in earnest, we made the decision to subsidize all ILL requests. If we offer Uncover, does the library pay or do patrons pay?

Capital District Library Council (CDLC) libraries can meet 90% of interlibrary loan requests among CDLC member libraries. I expect that percentage to decline because of all the cancellations among the member libraries. However, combined, the fiscal and human resources of CDLC libraries are tremendous. Utilizing them in a collaborative way is our challenge.

THOU SHALT FOSTER COMMUNICATION

It is difficult to separate communication from the other commandments, especially from education and involvement of faculty. Use every means available to communicate with faculty. Use your student newspaper and library newsletter. Send letters to all faculty, not just deans or administrators. Work with your Library Friends group and your faculty library committee. Get on the agenda of a faculty council/senate meeting. Speak individually with faculty members and administrators. I've had many conversations with both groups while walking in from the parking lot. There's a lot of misinformation out there. In a Faculty Council meeting, one faculty member announced that our problems with serial costs would be solved when all journals become electronic. Electronic doesn't mean free.

It's easy to call a faceless library person and yell and scream about serials cancellations. Become a name with a face. Work on campus committees with faculty. Let the faculty get to know you. Earn respect and credibility.

It's just as important to keep open lines of communication among libraries, publishers, and vendors. The fact that I have firm prices for half of Rensselaer's 1994 renewals is the result of the communication and work of the three groups. When you cancel a title, let the publisher and vendor know that you are canceling because the price is too high. At the 1989 Charleston Conference, the CEO of a major STM publisher said that libraries should maintain subscriptions and cut personnel, because personnel costs take up the largest part of a library's budget. I don't think you will hear a publisher say that today. We have all learned from each other.

The commandments are straight forward. They sound easy. But, as with any set of guidelines, following them is the hard part.

A LOOK INTO THE FUTURE

Only Shakespearean witches see the future clearly. In my not-so-crystal-clear ball, I see university administrators becoming more concerned over the fact that they provide faculty with the labs, the library, the staff and other resources to conduct their research. Yet, they have to pay exorbitant prices for the results published in journals. More and more will view library journals as a fiscal sink hole. More and more will support cooperative ventures, networks and consortia among libraries. Administrators will adopt access rather than acquisition of information. They will probably reach that conclusion before faculty.

State-wide networks for resource sharing will reach even the small public and school libraries. Accreditation agencies will look at the access libraries provide rather than the number of titles purchased and shelved in the stacks.

Faculty involved in research that is quickly dated will turn to electronic communication because of its speed and interactive nature. Faculty with similar interests will work together electronically. Research will become more dynamic in a multimedia environment. Slowly the tenure system will change to value and encourage quality over quantity.

Publishing will change as librarians and faculty continue to ask, "Why does a page in a commercially published journal cost four times as much as one in a society journal?" As the expensive titles are canceled and become less accessible, faculty will choose to publish in those titles which are found in libraries, the affordable titles. Core journals which are difficult to find will cease to be core and then cease entirely. Society publishers who have maintained their quality and kept costs down will flourish. The availability of campus computing resources and concerns about ownership of research results and copyright will encourage universities to venture into electronic publishing. And to the delight of Sandy Paul, standards will be embraced and used by all.

Libraries will emphasize access and share resources with each other. Some will participate in cooperative collection development. Most will rely in part on commercial document delivery services. Libraries will struggle with the issue, "Who pays for information?" Approaches will vary as libraries try to avoid creating a society of information haves and information havenots. Libraries will find preservation of electronic information for future generations another area of concern. Will today's technology be compatible with tomorrow's?

The silver lining in the serials pricing crisis is that we have been forced off of the road to extinction and onto the evolutionary path of library cooperation and resource sharing. My crystal ball may not be clear but it does show a dynamic, exciting, and challenging future for all of us.

NOTES

1. *Blackwell North America Approval Program Coverage and Cost Study 1987/88.* Lake Oswego: Blackwell North America, 1988.

2. Dougherty, Richard M. "And the Beat Goes On: The Continuing Crisis in Journal Subscription Prices." *Library Issues* 10, no. 6 (July 1990).

3. Kohl, David F. "OhioLINK: Plugging into Progress." *Library Journal* 118, no. 16 (October 1, 1993), pp. 42-46.

Index

© 1995 by The Haworth Press, Inc. All rights reserved.

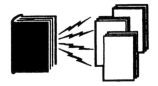

Haworth
DOCUMENT DELIVERY
SERVICE

This new service provides a single-article order form for any article from a Haworth journal.

- *Time Saving:* No running around from library to library to find a specific article.
- *Cost Effective:* All costs are kept down to a minimum.
- *Fast Delivery:* Choose from several options, including same-day FAX.
- *No Copyright Hassles:* You will be supplied by the original publisher.
- *Easy Payment:* Choose from several easy payment methods.

Open Accounts Welcome for ...
- Library Interlibrary Loan Departments
- Library Network/Consortia Wishing to Provide Single-Article Services
- Indexing/Abstracting Services with Single Article Provision Services
- Document Provision Brokers and Freelance Information Service Providers

MAIL or *FAX* THIS ENTIRE ORDER FORM TO:

Haworth Document Delivery Service
The Haworth Press, Inc.
10 Alice Street
Binghamton, NY 13904-1580

or FAX: (607) 722-6362
or CALL: 1-800-3-HAWORTH
(1-800-342-9678; 9am-5pm EST)

PLEASE SEND ME PHOTOCOPIES OF THE FOLLOWING SINGLE ARTICLES:

1) Journal Title: _____
    Vol/Issue/Year:_____Starting & Ending Pages:_____
    Article Title:_____

2) Journal Title: _____
    Vol/Issue/Year:_____Starting & Ending Pages:_____
    Article Title:_____

3) Journal Title: _____
    Vol/Issue/Year:_____Starting & Ending Pages:_____
    Article Title:_____

4) Journal Title: _____
    Vol/Issue/Year:_____Starting & Ending Pages:_____
    Article Title:_____

(See other side for Costs and Payment Information)

COSTS: Please figure your cost to order quality copies of an article.
1. Set-up charge per article: $8.00
   ($8.00 × number of separate articles) _____
2. Photocopying charge for each article:
   1-10 pages: $1.00 _____

   11-19 pages: $3.00 _____

   20-29 pages: $5.00 _____

   30+ pages: $2.00/10 pages _____
3. Flexicover (optional): $2.00/article _____
4. Postage & Handling: US: $1.00 for the first article/
   $.50 each additional article _____

   Federal Express: $25.00 _____

   Outside US: $2.00 for first article/
   $.50 each additional article _____
5. Same-day FAX service: $.35 per page _____

GRAND TOTAL: _____

METHOD OF PAYMENT: (please check one)
❑ Check enclosed   ❑ Please ship and bill. PO # _____
            (sorry we can ship and bill to bookstores only! All others must pre-pay)
❑ Charge to my credit card: ❑ Visa; ❑ MasterCard; ❑ American Express;

Account Number: _____ Expiration date: _____

Signature: ✗ _____

Name: _____ Institution: _____

Address: _____

_____

City: _____ State: _____ Zip: _____

Phone Number: _____ FAX Number: _____

MAIL or *FAX* THIS ENTIRE ORDER FORM TO:

Haworth Document Delivery Service	**or FAX:** (607) 722-6362
The Haworth Press, Inc.	**or CALL:** 1-800-3-HAWORTH
10 Alice Street	(1-800-342-9678; 9am-5pm EST)
Binghamton, NY 13904-1580	

3 0020 00150 9654